Georgina Fuggle trained at Leith's Cookery School and went on to work for Green & Black's for two years, practice as a food stylist, open one of the first pop-up restaurants in London (Hart & Fuggle) and then wind up as the senior food editor for a UK publishing house. She has now retreated to the English countryside where beautiful food is rife and there is green space aplenty.

TAKE ONE POT

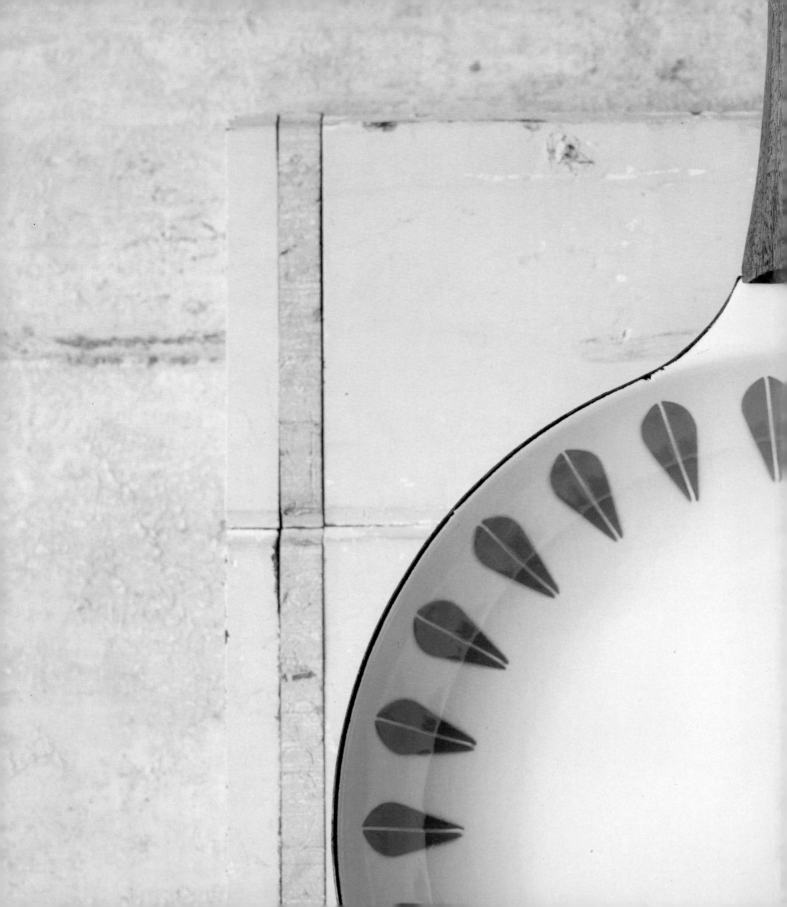

TAKE ONE POT

Super-simple recipes to
cook in one pot

GEORGINA
FUGGLE

....

Photography by

Tara Fisher

KYLE BOOKS

Published in 2013 by Kyle Books
www.kylebooks.com

Distributed by National Book Network
4501 Forbes Blvd., Suite 200
Lanham, MD 20706
Phone: (800) 462-6420
Fax: 1-800-338-4550
Customercare@nbnbooks.com

ISBN: 978-1-906868-94-9

10 9 8 7 6 5 4 3 2 1

Georgina Fuggle is hereby identified as the author of this work in accordance with section 77 of the Copyright, Designs and Patents Act 1988.

Photography: Tara Fisher
Design: Nicky Collings
Prop styling: Wei Tang
Food styling: Georgina Fuggle and Joss Herd
Project editor: Sophie Allen
Copy editor: Emily Hatchwell
Production: Gemma John and Nic Jones

Library of Congress Control Number: 2013940644

Color reproduction by Scanhouse
Printed and bound in China by C&C Offset Printing Co. Ltd

Thank you to Le Creuset and Staub for lending us their wonderful pots.

ACKNOWLEDGMENTS

I've had quite a clear list of children's names in my mind for some years now and it's a funny thing when you discover one has been stolen from you. Sophie, the most wonderful editor, had already named her beautiful boy with the name at the very top of my list, but I still couldn't help liking her. Thank you for gently steering me, Tuesday night suppers, and walking me to the coach stop. May there be many more conversations and lots more laughter.

Tara and Nicky have been instrumental—just imagine this book with no pictures and no clever design. It's been gorgeous to spend days shooting in Brixton, South London together, eating a few more pecan Danish than were really necessary.

Alice. You are a perfect friend and a real inspiration to me. Who else would think to send a birthday cake decorated with zero when I announced my pregnancy? I've loved all the things we've done together and look forward to future antics.

Hannah. You've tested and retested with the most infectious enthusiasm. I'm so grateful to you. And Sarah, I couldn't have hoped for a better assistant.

Oenone and Will have eaten far more than their fair share of one pots throughout swelteringly hot summer days and helped me rework and retest recipes until we all felt pleased. My lovely mother-in-law, Sue, has cooked any recipes I felt needed a second opinion and frequently made inconvenient changes to schedules to squeeze in a one pot. Far beyond the call of duty but very, very much appreciated.

It's quite humbling to think how many people have steered me along this path, but there is one in particular who deserves a very public thank you. My Momma has eaten little else but one-pot meals, she has driven all over north Norfolk, East of England in search of fresh dill weed, and learned to enjoy a pig cheek or two. She has always said my pots are delicious. She has always gone above and beyond. Thank you.

Julia, Rachel, Henrietta, Annabel, and Rosie tested and fed their families with the results! I hope they were happy. You are all heroes.

And Nicko. You are endlessly encouraging and the person I would like most to share my table with. You are the Fuggle to my heart.

CONTENTS

ONE POT, PERIOD.

My mind takes a few minutes to rouse in the morning. If I'm good I wake and say a quick prayer before deciding what to eat for breakfast. If I'm bad I just decide what I can eat for breakfast. Talking, writing, and tasting food is how many of my hours are spent and still I delight in cooking like an enthusiastic honeybee.

The delight began when I was just a girl; a yard sale had been advertised, two weeks on Saturday in the village hall parking lot. Others scrabbled around their bedrooms gathering treasure while I buzzed around the kitchen baking plump cheese straws and currant scones. Our wares were packaged up, each of them costing but a few pennies, and we set sail for the elusive stall. I remember our profit being just a few pounds, but to me, an impressionable 12-year-old, this was the launch into professional cooking that I so desperately wanted.

Years passed, cooking methods were explored, and preferences formed, but it was a Christmas gift of a chrome black Le Creuset that ignited fervor for the one pot. Home was a minuscule apartment in Waterloo where there was absolutely no space for a food processor or a microwave. A sink, an oven, a tiny utensils drawer, and my huge black pot made up the bulk of a very cherished kitchen.

Practice makes perfect, we've all been told, and practice I did. Inspired by the classics but pushed forward by a London food scene bursting on my doorstep, I cooked long into the night. It was quite usual to be woken by the buzz of an alarm clock disturbing sleep to turn off a simmering stew. Then I would sneak back to bed, choosing to ignore the water, heat, steam, fury, and grease all over my beloved kitchen.

May I present to you my findings, my scrapbook of beloved one pots, each of which has been tasted and tested and has triumphed on the table. Each of which I hope will make you happy.

A FEW TIPS I'VE LEARNED ALONG THE WAY

Sharp Knives

These are actually far safer to use than their blunt cousins; they glide through ingredients rather than needing to be forced with excess pressure, so reduce emergency trips to locate adhesive bandage (or even your nearest ER). Ask your local butcher to help keep your set sharp—most of them will happily oblige.

Brown Your Meat Thoroughly

Few cooks realize how long it takes to brown meat thoroughly, but the process is, in my opinion, the most important stage of stews. Be patient; control the heat as best you can. A good rule of thumb is: if it's brown, flavor has developed; if it's black, the pot is in danger of tasting a bit bitter.

Oven Thermometer

Years of being a food editor taught me that ovens have different responses to being told to preheat to certain temperatures. A thermometer is worth its weight in gold when you're following a recipe, particularly one that involves a dish that sits in the oven for a good few hours.

Preparation, Preparation, Preparation

Most stews benefit from a day or two just sitting, getting to know themselves a bit better. If you have friends coming over, make the stew in advance so you have less to do on the day. Both the chef and the pot will be more content.

Liquids

I learned that anything is better than water in a stew. Don't throw away bottles of anything. If the wine is too dismal to be drunk at the table, it can be used to cut through oil for a salad dressing or top up stock in a recipe. For stock, use bouillon cubes if you have to, but most supermarkets stock a more upscale version in the form of pouches or tubs. If you haven't time to make homemade stock, these are your best bet.

Don't Rush

Most of my pots simmer at low temperature for a bit longer than it may take to pick up a sandwich at Starbucks, but they are worth the wait. Allow the meat to grow tender in its own time; if it's not falling apart, sit back and have another glass of wine while you wait.

The All-Important Pot

I'm not a food snob, I promise. There has been many a happy occasion when a good takeout has been coveted and, let's face it, enjoyed. However, I do, occasionally, raise my nose at people's cooking pots. Pasta, potatoes, rice, noodles—anything you can think of—enjoys having some room to boil. Always use a size bigger than you think is needed.

A heavy, iron-bottom pot will make your life easier, as you can sauté and stew in the very same one and it means less dishwashing, so smiles all round!

What to Stock Up On

There is little more satisfying than conjuring a fabulous meal from your very own pantry. Avoiding any trawl to the grocery store makes me feel like I've achieved, ticked the "organized mother" bracket, and my ego can be indulged with a proverbial pat on the back. But alas, too often, my kitchen cabinets have let me down at the critical, post-work, hypoglycemic moment when babies are screaming and a friend has just called to confirm that "dinner is on?"

So, what should those dreaded cabinets contain to help you along the one-pot highway?

Sea Salt—The crunch is glorious and the flavor intensifies any stew, soup, or chocolate pot. As much as salt shakers have their purpose, very rarely do they do the job as quickly or efficiently as a healthy hand pinch of sea salt.

Premium Canned Diced Tomatoes—Yes, you can buy cheap, watery tomatoes, but if your recipe requires just one can, and the tomatoes should actually be tasted, then do invest in your pantry and stock up on some good-quality canned tomatoes. I can't tell you exactly when they will rescue you during a culinary breakdown, but they will, I'm sure of it.

Olive oil—There are certainly moments for vegetable oil among recipes, but equally there are times when your ingredients deserve to be coated in gold. Extra virgin olive oil is indeed worth the expense, especially when it's the final drizzle over a dish before it reaches the table.

Onions—The backbone to a stew, onions need to be treated with the utmost respect. Occasionally I have asked for them to be flash-fried, thrown into boiling oil until their edges curl, but more often they should be gently, sympathetically cooked over lower heat for a few more minutes.

Dark Brown Sugar—It's both the caramel brown color and the complex caramel taste that pushes me to use just a touch of brown sugar in savory recipes. Often it can take the edge off a bitter onion or tart alcoholic taste.

MOTHER SOUPERIA

As a bishop's daughter, the title of this particular chapter resonates with my homegrown self. I think sitting among pews in a church nourishes the soul in a similar way to a hearty bowl of soup.

The recipes are simple; the pots generally look after themselves. The fine line between a soup and a stew is very nearly crossed in a number of the following recipes, but a chunky soup can be exactly what is needed following a grueling day at work or a bracing winter walk. Equally, an elegant beet number can kickstart a dinner party in an oh-so-sophisticated fashion. The choice is yours.

BEET & ORANGE SOUP
WITH SOUR CREAM

This dish is one of my favorites, developing the humble, earth-dwelling beet into a recipe fit for a king, with velvety texture, complexity of flavors, not to mention regal purple color. These majestic features are enhanced by an acidic splash of orange and a smooth scoop of sour cream, which completes the transformation from rags to riches.

PREP TIME 15 MINUTES   SERVES 6   COOK TIME 1½ HOURS

1 tablespoon vegetable oil

2 red onions, coarsely chopped

3 huge garlic cloves, peeled and finely sliced

2 celery stalks, coarsely chopped

½ teaspoon ground cinnamon

18 ounces beets, peeled and cut into ½- to ¾-inch cubes

5 cups hot vegetable stock

Grated and thinly pared zest and juice of 1 large orange

Sea salt and freshly ground black pepper

6 spoonfuls of sour cream, to serve

1 In a large saucepan, heat the vegetable oil and add the onions, garlic, and celery. Cook, covered, on very very gentle heat until the vegetables are soft and panting from exhaustion, 15 minutes; add the cinnamon for the final 5 minutes. Stir every so often to make sure nothing is turning to coal.

2 Add the cubed beet to the pot and cook until it begins to soften, 5 to 10 minutes. Pour over the hot stock, season well, then cover and simmer until the beet is tender and cuts like butter, about 1 hour.

3 Use a hand blender or food processor to puree the soup in batches until smooth. Try to avoid turning your kitchen purple! Return the soup to the saucepan and stir through the fresh orange juice. Anoint with the cold sour cream and a sprinkling of grated and thinly pared orange zest before serving.

LEEK, KALE
& BARLEY BROTH

Inexpensive food can be beautiful food and this is a fine example of that. Pearl barley has a nutty, unassuming sort of taste and is a perfect "filler" in a fall-type soup like this one. I've cooked it in chicken stock, as I think it has a slightly punchier flavor, but of course you could switch to vegetable stock and make it teetotal vegetarian.

PREP TIME 15 MINUTES · MAKES 6 TO 8 MUGFULS · COOK TIME 50 MINUTES

2 tablespoons olive oil

2 medium leeks, finely sliced

4 garlic cloves, peeled and sliced

3 sprigs of thyme

½ cup dry pearl barley

2 quarts hot chicken stock

7 ounces kale, stems removed, washed thoroughly, and coarsely chopped

2 tablespoons coarsely chopped flat-leaf parsley

Sea salt and freshly ground black pepper

FOR THE SALTED PAPRIKA YOGURT

¾ heaping cup crème fraîche or Greek yogurt

Grated zest of 1 lemon and juice of ½ lemon

½ teaspoon Spanish smoked paprika

2 good pinches of sea salt

1 In a large, deep saucepan, heat the olive oil, add the leeks and garlic, and cook over medium heat until the leeks have begun to turn translucent, but don't allow them to color, 2 to 3 minutes.

2 Add the sprigs of thyme and season well. Cover and continue to cook on very low heat until the leeks have wilted, 10 minutes, stirring occasionally to stop anything catching on the bottom of the pan. Stir the pearl barley into the pot and pour over the hot chicken stock. Simmer gently until the barley is tender, 30 to 40 minutes.

3 Stir in the kale toward the end of the cooking time and let boil for 6 to 8 minutes. Top up with a little more hot stock if you think it's needed. It's lovely for the kale to retain some of its crunch and vibrant green, so don't cook it for longer than needed.

4 For the salted paprika yogurt, simply combine the crème fraîche, lemon zest, juice, paprika, and salt and let sit while the soup develops.

5 Ladle into the mugs and serve your soup with parsley bobbing in it and a good heap of paprika yogurt.

POTATO, PROSCIUTTO
& ROSEMARY SOUP

There is a fine line between a chunky soup and a light stew and this recipe could fall into either camp. Very simple ingredients create a frugal soup that pretty much takes care of itself. Just drop everything in and let the saucepan do the hard work.

....

PREP TIME 10 MINUTES   SERVES 6   COOK TIME 35 MINUTES

....

3 tablespoons butter

1 large onion, coarsely chopped

½ tablespoon finely chopped rosemary

1¼ pounds mealy potatoes, peeled and cut into
   ¾-inch dice

3⅓ cups hot chicken stock

¾ cup milk

6 slices of prosciutto, torn into slithers

A little cream, to finish

Sea salt and freshly ground black pepper

1 In a heavy-bottom saucepan, melt the butter over medium heat. Reduce the heat to low and add the onion, rosemary, and potato chunks, stirring gently. Season well, cover with a lid, and let the vegetables soften without coloring, about 12 minutes. Give the saucepan a good shake halfway through to prevent anything catching on the bottom.

2 Add the stock and milk to the pan, stir thoroughly, and continue to cook until the potatoes are falling apart, another 20 minutes. Puree the soup in a blender or using a hand blender.

3 Give the soup a good taste to make sure the seasoning is correct and serve with slithers of prosciutto and cream balancing on the surface.

FISH SOUP
WITH A TOUCH OF THE EAST

Nothing prepares an English girl for the perils of Thai backstreets. Incessant honking, oppressive heat, and street vendor carts showcasing Pad Thai and deep-fried crabs paint a vivid picture of a vibrant country. I remember the smell of fresh lime and cilantro bouncing from pots and brothy noodles being slurped by the locals. This fish soup reminds me of those warm days and can be a welcome escape from bleak weather.

PREP TIME 15 MINUTES   SERVES 4   COOK TIME 30 MINUTES

1 teaspoon sunflower oil

2 garlic cloves, peeled and diced

5 cups fish stock

2 small Thai chiles, finely chopped

2 lemongrass stalks, bruised and cut in half lengthwise

A few cilantro stems, finely chopped

2-inch piece of fresh ginger, peeled and finely chopped

1⅔ cups coconut milk

10½ ounces raw jumbo shrimp, peeled and deveined but with tails still attached

9 ounces salmon fillet, cut into bite-size pieces

¼ pound snow peas, each sliced in half on the diagonal

Juice of 1 lime

2 teaspoons fish sauce

Cilantro leaves

1 In a large saucepan, heat the oil and add the garlic. Sauté over medium heat for a couple of minutes, then pour the fish stock into the pan. Bring to a boil and add the chiles, lemongrass, cilantro stems, and ginger. Reduce the stock to a simmer and let the ingredients infuse for 15 minutes.

2 Carefully fish out the lemongrass and pour in the coconut milk. Bring to a simmer before adding the shrimp, salmon, and snow peas. Cook just until the fish is opaque and cooked through, about 2 minutes. Finally, stir in the lime juice and fish sauce. Serve with a delicate bundle of cilantro leaves and eat instantly.

BORLOTTI BEAN
TOMATO & SAGE SOUP

Most recipes for Italian-style tomato soup stand out with their basic technique of creating a *soffritto*, a simple melange of olive oil, celery, carrots, and onion. This makes a wonderfully strong foundation to the soup upon which many ingredients can be added. Here is just one idea, which happens to include my favorite bean. Eat with chunks of crusty bread, preferably while sitting on the couch wrapped in a fleece.

PREP TIME 20 MINUTES   SERVES 6   COOK TIME 1 HOUR

6 tablespoons olive oil

3 celery stalks, finely diced

2 carrots, peeled and finely diced

1 medium onion, finely diced

2 garlic cloves, peeled and finely chopped

5 or 6 sage leaves, coarsely chopped, plus extra leaves
   to garnish

1 tablespoon tomato paste

2¼ pounds brilliant-quality tomatoes, coarsely chopped
   into chunks

3⅓ cups vegetable stock

1 (14- to 15-ounce) can borlotti (cranberry) beans,
   drained and rinsed

1 In a 3-quart casserole dish, heat the olive oil over medium heat. Add the celery, carrots, onion, garlic, and chopped sage, reduce the heat to low, and gently sauté until the vegetables have softened, about 15 minutes, stirring occasionally. Try not to get any color on the vegetables, as this is a gentle cooking process.

2 Add the tomato paste and stir in before adding the chopped tomatoes. Turn the heat to low and cook, covered, for an additional 15 minutes, wiggling the pan every few minutes to prevent anything catching on the bottom. Pour over the stock and bring to a boil. Simmer for 30 minutes without a lid.

3 Using a hand blender, puree about half of the soup so you are still left with some delicious chunks. Stir in the beans and cook until your soup is heated through and the beans are warm, about 2 minutes. Garnish with deep-fried sage leaves (see tip).

 TIP—DEEP-FRIED SAGE LEAVES MAKE A QUICK AND DELICATE GARNISH FOR THIS SOUP. SIMPLY, IN A PAN, HEAT A COUPLE OF TABLESPOONS OF OIL UNTIL HOT, THEN DROP THE LEAVES IN FOR A FEW SECONDS. REMOVE THE LEAVES, DRAIN ON PAPER TOWELS, AND SPRINKLE WITH SALT.

CHILLY AVOCADO
CUCUMBER & YOGURT SOUP

Some might indulge in a spa visit to have cucumber slices laid on their eyes while whale music is played in the background, but my suggestion would be to save the money and rustle up the following. It's relaxingly simple, packed with all the right vitamins, and, as the expression goes, "cool as a cucumber."

PREP TIME 15 MINUTES   **ENOUGH FOR 6 SMALL BOWLS**   COOK TIME 5 MINUTES

1 tablespoon butter

1 onion, coarsely chopped

2 garlic cloves, peeled and squashed

1 quart cold vegetable stock

1 cucumber, peeled, chopped, and the seeds scooped out

1 large very ripe avocado or 2 smaller ones, peeled, pitted, and coarsely chopped

3 tablespoons chopped mint

1 cup thick Greek yogurt

A few drops of Tabasco (optional)

Sea salt and freshly ground black pepper

A handful of ice cubes and mint leaves, to serve

1 In a heavy-bottomed saucepan, melt the butter and add the onion. Cook over gentle heat until softened but not colored, a few minutes. Add the garlic to the pot and cook for another minute.

2 Remove from the heat and add the cold stock, cucumber chunks, avocado, and chopped mint. Simply puree using a hand blender or food processor—now you see how easy it is.

3 Stir through the Greek yogurt until you reach your desired creaminess. Season to taste and add the Tabasco if you fancy a bit of heat.

4 Serve in bowls over ice cubes and garnish with mint leaves. Now all you need is for the sun to come out.

APPLE & PARSNIP
SOUP

There is something effortlessly comforting about apples and parsnips; here they are combined in an elegant partnership perfect for a fall lunch. Do try the parsnip chips, as they are the proverbial "icing on the cake" and will provide an excellent and decorative use for the skin. Waste not, want not, as my father would say.

PREP TIME 25 MINUTES   **MAKES 4 BIG BOWLS OR 6 GIRLIE PORTIONS**   COOK TIME 1 HOUR 10 MINUTES

1 tablespoon salted butter

1 large onion, coarsely chopped

1 teaspoon ground cumin

A trickle of honey

26 ounces parsnips (about 5), peeled and cut into ¾-inch dice (keep the peelings for the chips)

1 medium potato, peeled and cut into ¾-inch dice

2 healthy-size green apples, peeled, cored, and cut into ¾-inch dice

5 cups vegetable stock

Plain yogurt or parsnip chips (see tip below), to serve

Sea salt and freshly ground black pepper

1 In a 3-quart saucepan, melt the butter over gentle heat. Add the onion and cumin and sauté until the onion is translucent, about 2 minutes. Stir in the honey and let bubble for a few moments.

2 Add the parsnip, potato, and apple chunks and stir so all the pieces are coated in the cumin honey.

3 Pour over the hot vegetable stock and let simmer, covered, for an hour. Stir occasionally to make sure your soup is cooking evenly.

4 When everything is soft and the vegetables cut like butter, simply puree using a hand blender. If you like the soup thinner, loosen with either milk or hot water. Add a good pinch of salt and a grating of black pepper. Return to the stove to heat through and then serve with a good spoonful of yogurt or some parsnip chips.

TIP—TO MAKE THE PARSNIP CHIPS, SIMPLY POUR APPROXIMATELY 3 TABLESPOONS VEGETABLE OIL INTO A DEEP SKILLET. HEAT OVER HIGH HEAT AND ADD THE PARSNIP PEELINGS. SPRINKLE A GENEROUS AMOUNT OF SALT OVER THE PEELINGS AND LET SIZZLE. DON'T BE TEMPTED TO MOVE THEM AROUND TOO MUCH—JUST EVERY MINUTE OR SO. THEY SHOULD TAKE 4 TO 5 MINUTES TO CRISP UP. DRAIN ON PAPER TOWELS AND THROW A GOOD BUNDLE ON TOP OF THE SOUP.

JUST VEGGIES

I was once told this old story that makes me smile. A young undergraduate was starting at Cambridge University. He and his fellow students arrived on day one to be met by a frosty-looking matron, who laid down a few ground rules to the boys: "Now listen here," she bellowed, "I will tolerate, every once in a while, you bringing girls back to your rooms. I will even turn a blind eye if you bring a man back to your room, but what I absolutely can't abide is vegetarians."

Luckily I don't share this opinion; in fact, vegetarian food is to be relished. I hope you enjoy the following clutch of recipes, some of which take moments, while others require a wee bit of planning, but all, I promise, are delicious.

POLENTA BAKE
WITH TOMATO, FETA & MUSHROOMS

Years ago, ground polenta simply provided hunger-defying gruel to the poor, but today it's found cooked with the expensive additions of Parmesan and butter. The transformation has put it back on the map of Michelin-starred menus and into the repertoire of enthusiastic cooks. Here, instant polenta is used, so there are only minutes from package to plate and the peasant price tag still holds strong. It's well worth stocking a package in your pantry.

PREP TIME 10 MINUTES   SERVES 6   COOK TIME 20 MINUTES

1 cup instant polenta

3 tablespoons unsalted butter, cut into chunks

3¼ cups hot vegetable stock

⅔ cup finely grated Parmesan cheese

1½ cups thinly sliced mushrooms (any type really;
   my preference would be mini portobello)

1 cup cherry tomatoes, some halved, some not

⅔ cup crumbled feta cheese

A handful of delicate arugula

Sea salt and freshly ground black pepper

1 Preheat your broiler to high.

2 Put the polenta and chunks of butter in a deep, 10-inch-diameter ovenproof skillet over medium heat. Gradually pour the hot stock onto the polenta, beating with gusto to prevent any large lumps forming. Keep beating until the mixture has thickened and is starting to bubble like erupting volcanoes, about 4 to 5 minutes. Season well with black pepper and salt.

3 Remove the pan from the heat and stir through the Parmesan. You could clean the sides of your skillet at this stage to remove any obvious volcano larva (spitting polenta). Top the polenta with the mushroom slices, tomatoes, and crumbled feta.

4 Put the pan under the hot broiler until the tomato skins have burst and the mushrooms have wilted with the heat, 10 to 12 minutes. Let cool for a few minutes before dressing with arugula to serve.

 TIP—YOU WILL SEE PARMESAN HAS BEEN USED TO ADD FLAVOR, BUT OF COURSE ANY FULL-FLAVORED CHEESE WOULD BE DELICIOUS. USE A VEGETARIAN VARIETY IF YOU'RE ABLE TO TRACK IT DOWN.

PEARLED SPELT RISOTTO
WITH WATERCRESS & LEMON

There is a certain thrill to discovering fresh watercress swimming in a docile river, gesturing the beginning of spring. It is so green, peppery, and robust that it can stand out by itself. Here, we have a simple spelt risotto in which the watercress is the star of the show. I'd eat it with a chunky wedge of garlic bread.

PREP TIME 10 MINUTES   SERVES 4   COOK TIME 30 MINUTES

2 tablespoons (¼ stick) butter

1 tablespoon olive oil

1 onion, finely chopped

2 garlic cloves, peeled and finely chopped

1 cup dry pearled spelt (alternatively, use risotto rice)

½ cup dry white wine

1 quart hot vegetable stock

1 (3-ounce) bunch of watercress, washed and coarsely chopped

Grated zest and juice of 1 lemon

½ cup grated Parmesan cheese

Sea salt and freshly ground black pepper

A few rounds of goat cheese, to serve

1 In a large saucepan, heat half of the butter and all of the oil, add the onion and garlic, and sauté over low heat, stirring occasionally, until softened, about 5 minutes. Add the pearled spelt (or risotto rice) and stir for 1 minute until the grains are coated in the buttery oil.

2 Pour in the wine and simmer over high heat until nearly all has evaporated. A word of warning: there are times for drinking alcohol, but not within a risotto—take the time to let the alcohol evaporate.

3 Reduce the heat to gentle and begin to add the hot stock, a ladleful at a time, letting each ladleful be absorbed before adding the next. Keep adding the stock and stirring continuously until all of the liquid has been absorbed. This will take 18 to 20 minutes.

4 Remove the risotto from the heat and add the remaining butter, the chopped watercress, lemon zest and juice, and the Parmesan. Stir until the watercress has just wilted, check for seasoning, and then serve with a round or two of goat cheese resting on top.

BASIL, NUTMEG
& RICOTTA CANNELLONI

Fresh pasta used to be confined to specialist delis, served only by olive-skinned Italians, but, as they often do, supermarkets have made this ingredient accessible to all of us. The recipe here forges strong Italian ingredients to create a dish that can only be described as "*molto bene.*"

PREP TIME 30 MINUTES · · · · · · · · **SERVES 6** · · · · · · · · COOK TIME 1 HOUR

2 cups drained fresh ricotta cheese

A good (1-ounce) bunch of basil

½ nutmeg, grated, or 1 teaspoon ground nutmeg

½ cup grated Parmesan cheese

½ pound fresh Italian vine tomatoes, coarsely chopped

3 cups strained tomatoes (the more homemade, the better)

9 ounces fresh pasta sheets

4 to 5 scallions, finely chopped

Sea salt and freshly ground black pepper

1 Preheat the oven to 350°F.

2 In a large bowl, gently combine the ricotta, basil, nutmeg, half of the Parmesan, and the coarsely chopped tomatoes. Season well. Pour half of the strained tomatoes into the bottom of a 2-quart ovenproof dish.

3 Cut the pasta sheets into individual rectangles (approximately 5 x 4 inches)—don't worry too much if they aren't these exact measurements, as every pasta sheet varies in size. Lay these rectangles on your counter like a patchwork blanket and put 2 heaping tablespoons of the ricotta mixture along one edge of each rectangle. Roll up and place in your dish, join-side down to secure them. Continue until you have used all of the filling and pasta sheets. It doesn't matter if you have to pile them up a bit, but make sure the bottom layer is snug.

4 Cover with the remaining strained tomatoes and sprinkle over the scallions and the rest of the Parmesan. Give the dish a good grating of black pepper. Cover with greased foil and bake for 1 hour.

ORZO WITH MINT
& SUN-DRIED TOMATOES

Orzo is a tiny rice-shaped pasta traditionally used in Italian soups, but it's very versatile and cooks in minutes. I've used it here in a warm salad, and given it a bit more oomph by adding sun-dried tomatoes and mint. This dish will be on your table faster than it takes to call for a takeout.

PREP TIME 5 MINUTES   SERVES 4   COOK TIME 20 MINUTES

1¾ cups dry orzo

½ cup cream cheese

5½ ounces young spinach leaves

A (1-ounce) bunch of mint, chopped (reserve a
   few whole leaves for garnish)

½ cup sun-dried tomatoes, coarsely chopped

Sea salt and freshly ground black pepper

1 Heat a large pot of boiling water and drop the orzo into the water. Stir vigorously at once, to prevent the little grains sticking, and then stir occasionally during cooking. Simmer for 8 minutes. Scoop out ⅓ cup of the cooking water and set aside.

2 Drain the orzo and return to the pot with the reserved cooking water. Keep the pot over very gentle heat while you add the cream cheese and spinach leaves. Stir until the spinach has wilted and the cheese has coated the grains. Add the chopped mint and sun-dried tomatoes. Season with salt and freshly ground black pepper.

3 Serve with a fresh mint leaf or two over the top.

FRESHLY GRATED
ASIAN SALAD

Nothing is as virtuous as an Asian salad: fresh, crunchy vegetables tossed lightly with a tangy dressing and embellished with roasted peanuts. A friend, Belle, taught me how to fashion Asian cuisine from weathered English ingredients, so I have her to thank for this refreshing dish.

PREP TIME 20 MINUTES   SERVES 4

14 ounces cucumber

1 red bell pepper, cut into the thinnest strips possible

1½ cups bean sprouts

1 large carrot, peeled and grated

1 teaspoon fish sauce

1 tablespoon rice vinegar

2 tablespoons vegetable oil

1 tablespoon seriously finely chopped lemongrass

3 tablespoons lime juice

1 tablespoon jaggery (palm sugar) or dark brown sugar

1 tablespoon finely chopped mint, plus extra leaves
   to garnish

⅓ cup chopped roasted peanuts

1 First, prepare the cucumber. Cut it in half lengthwise, then scoop out the seeds (I find a teaspoon does the best job of this) and discard. Cut each hollowed length into three equal chunks and then each chunk into thin strips. Toss with the red bell pepper strips, bean sprouts, and grated carrot and set aside.

2 To make the dressing, put the fish sauce, rice vinegar, vegetable oil, lemongrass, lime juice, sugar, and chopped mint in a small bowl and stir to combine, or shake together in a closed clean screwtop jar.

3 Put all the ingredients except the peanuts in a large bowl and toss together. Sprinkle over the dressing and dust with the chopped peanuts. Job done.

COUNTRYSIDE POT

PREP TIME 10 MINUTES • COOK TIME 25 MINUTES

Salads have moved on a long way since the days of a limp Caesar or Niçoise. Forgive me—these recipes are wonderful for the correct moment, but with the wealth of seasonal ingredients available, it's fitting that salads can meander down many different paths. Here we have a hearty salad, a rugby player's equivalent of the traditional green side, which requires only a chunk of dripping Brie and a generous dollop of chutney.

SERVES 4 TO 6

2¼ pounds new potatoes, the bigger ones cut in half

7 ounces green beans, trimmed

2 (14- to 15-ounce) cans borlotti (cranberry) beans, drained and rinsed

1 red onion, sliced into thin slivers

A good handful of flat-leaf parsley, coarsely chopped

Grated zest of 1 lemon

FOR THE DRESSING

2 tablespoons Dijon mustard

½ cup olive oil

4 tablespoons cider vinegar

2 teaspoons granulated sugar

1 Put the potatoes in a saucepan of cold water and bring to a simmer. Cook until tender, approximately 20 minutes. Add the green beans to the pan for the last 3 to 4 minutes so they are just tender but still with a little crunch.

2 Make your dressing: combine all the ingredients and stir, or shake, until perfectly emulsified.

3 Drain the beans and potatoes. Return to the pan and stir through the beans, red onion, and dressing. Sprinkle over the parsley and lemon zest and serve.

PANZANELLA

PREP TIME 45 MINUTES

Panzanella is the salad world's response to bread recycling. Don't discard aged loaves as if they are models teetering on the age of thirty; in fact, the slightly drier the bread, the better the salad. Watch as the ciabatta soaks up freshly escaped tomato juice and a tart red wine vinegar dressing to become a scrumptious base to this summer recipe.

SERVES 4

10½ ounces 1- or 2-day-old bread (ciabatta is best)

3 ripe beefsteak tomatoes

1 small red onion, finely chopped

2 garlic cloves, peeled and crushed

1 medium cucumber, chopped into quarters lengthwise, then sliced

A handful of caper berries

4 tablespoons extra virgin olive oil

4 tablespoons red wine vinegar

1 ball of tender buffalo mozzarella, torn into bite-size chunks

A handful of basil and mint leaves

Sea salt and freshly ground black pepper

1 Tear or cube the bread into ¾- to 1¼-inch chunks and put into a large bowl. Coarsely chop the tomatoes, reserving all the lovely juices that try to run away, and add to the bowl with the onion, garlic, cucumber, and caper berries. Toss lightly to combine and evenly distribute all the ingredients.

2 Mix together the olive oil and vinegar, then pour over the bread and tomato mixture. Let sit for 20 minutes in the fridge so all the flavors have a chance to socialize.

3 Just before serving, toss through the mozzarella, basil, and mint leaves. Season and serve, preferably when you are on vacation in Italy, or want to be!

BULGUR WHEAT
BEET & AVOCADO SALAD

Beets are having a renaissance and why shouldn't they? Their intense color, earthy flavor, and remarkable health properties have put them firmly on the superfoods map. If eating beets raw, just scrub clean, grate as you would a carrot, and forget any distant memories of jarred, pickled beets that may cloud your opinion. Catch the beets before they wrinkle and the skin turns into that of an old man; you've got about a week before they start looking sad.

PREP TIME 20 MINUTES   **SERVES 4 TO 6**   COOK TIME 15 MINUTES

1 cup dry bulgur wheat

18 ounces raw beets (approx. 4), peeled or
    aggressively scrubbed

2 ripe avocados, peeled, pitted, and sliced

1 red onion, finely sliced

4 tablespoons chopped dill weed

4 tablespoons extra virgin olive oil

3 tablespoons white wine vinegar

½ teaspoon granulated sugar

½ teaspoon Tabasco

1 teaspoon whole grain mustard

1 Put the bulgur wheat in a small pan with 2½ cups cold water. Bring to a boil and then simmer for 12 to 15 minutes. Drain and fork through the grains to make sure you haven't got any nasty clumps.

2 Cut the beets as you wish. You could, for example, grate them, use the matchstick chopper on a food processor, or use your knife skills to slice them into matchsticks by hand. One piece of advice is to use rubber gloves to prevent unwanted stains on your hands.

3 Lightly toss together the bulgur wheat, beet, avocados, red onion, and dill weed. In a small pitcher, combine the olive oil, vinegar, sugar, Tabasco, and mustard. Drizzle the dressing over the salad, which is now ready to serve (but not to anybody wearing white!).

RICOTTA & WHITE BEAN MEDLEY

PREP TIME 15 MINUTES

My sister Caroline gets married this year and we've had many crucial conversations about the implications of a white or off-white wedding dress. This dish made me think of her. Startling white ricotta clouds are tossed with golden-white cannellini beans, each competing to catch the eye. Other summer ingredients are the sunshine backdrop to a jolly simple yet scrumptious dish.

SERVES 4

1 (14- to 15-ounce) can cannellini beans, drained and rinsed

3 to 4 scallions, sliced on the diagonal

1 cup cherry tomatoes, halved

1 large red chile, seeded and finely sliced

½ cup black olives, pitted

3 tablespoons olive oil

2 tablespoons balsamic vinegar

3½ ounces pea shoots (dau miu)

Scant ½ cup drained fresh ricotta cheese

Sea salt and freshly ground black pepper

1 In a large bowl, lightly toss the cannellini beans, scallions, tomatoes, chile, and olives. Drizzle over the olive oil and balsamic vinegar and toss to coat.

2 Gently add the pea shoots, handling them like thin glass to try to avoid bruising the leaves.

3 Arrange in a lovely dish and spoon the ricotta over the salad. Punctuate with salt and pepper and serve.

GOAT CHEESE & SCALLION FETTUCCINE

PREP TIME 10 MINUTES • COOK TIME 15 MINUTES

One Sunday morning four of us embarked on a significant ten-mile run, along the paved roads from Waterloo, Central London to London Fields, East London. The reward was a lengthy swim in the outdoor pool and this lunch on our return home.

SERVES 4

18 ounces dry fettuccine

3 tablespoons very soft butter

½ cup finely grated Parmesan cheese

3 ounces creamy, rindless goat cheese

A large bunch of scallions, finely chopped on the diagonal

1 heaping cup hazelnuts, toasted until a little charred

Sea salt and freshly ground black pepper

1 First point. Read through the recipe. This one is quick, but it relies on you being organized! Don't cook the pasta until you have all the sauce ingredients ready to go.

2 Bring a large pot of water to a boil. When the water starts to simmer, drop the pasta in and cook according to the package directions just until al dente. Be careful not to overcook the pasta: this dish needs a little bite to it. While the pasta is cooking, scoop out ¾ cup of the cooking water and keep aside.

3 Drain the pasta thoroughly, then return the empty pot to low heat. Working quickly, add the reserved water, softened butter, Parmesan, goat cheese, and scallions (reserving a few for the garnish). Cook over medium heat for a minute or so, stirring continuously, until the cheese and butter coat the pasta. Season well with salt and black pepper. Remove the pot from the heat and stir in the hazelnuts. Serve right away, garnished with the reserved scallions.

PERFECTLY PUFFED
CHEESE & BREAD POT

My Canadian friend Andrea taught me this recipe. Her mom used to make it on Christmas Day morning, to be eaten bleary-eyed amid the excitement, bursting stockings, and chilled champagne. Everything should be prepared the night before so the humble ingredients have time to mingle and be transformed from a relatively ordinary cluster into an exceptionally yummy dish. The magic of Christmas perhaps?

PREP TIME 20 MINUTES
(PLUS OVERNIGHT SOAKING)

SERVES 6

COOK TIME 50 MINUTES

2 tablespoons (¼ stick) very soft butter, plus extra
    for greasing
4 to 6 slices of white bread (¾- to 1¼-inches thick),
    crusts removed (approx. 5½ ounces crustless weight)

Scant 1 cup shredded sharp cheddar cheese
2 medium free-range eggs
1¼ cups lowfat milk
Sea salt and freshly ground black pepper

1 Grease a 1-quart ovenproof soufflé dish; I always find my fingers the most useful implement to do this with.

2 Spread the slices of bread with the softened butter, then cut into approx. 1¼-inch cubes. There should be enough to fill the soufflé dish three-quarters full. Place in the dish, add the shredded cheddar, and, using your hands, combine so the cheese is evenly distributed.

3 Crack the eggs into a small bowl and beat lightly using a wire whip. Add the milk and beat for 2 to 3 minutes. Season well. Slowly pour over the bread-and-cheese mixture. Cover and pop in the fridge overnight.

4 All the hard work has been done. The next day, all that's needed is to preheat the oven to 400°F and bake the soufflé for 40 minutes, or until golden and puffed like a peacock.

SWEET POTATO
& COCONUT DHAL

Whoever said lentils were bland? With the addition of just a few delicate spices, this recipe makes for a beautifully aromatic and chunky dhal: a delicious accompaniment for a curry or a simple lunch to take to the office. Be sure to transform yours with a generous spoonful of Greek yogurt and some torn cilantro; after all, even a simple dhal deserves to be dressed for the table.

PREP TIME 15 MINUTES
(PLUS OVERNIGHT SOAKING)

SERVES 6 (SIDE) OR 4 (MAIN)

COOK TIME 1 HOUR

Scant 1 cup dry yellow split peas

1 tablespoon olive oil

1 onion, finely chopped

½ teaspoon crushed red pepper

1 teaspoon garam masala

1 teaspoon ground turmeric

1 teaspoon ground cumin

1¼-inch piece of fresh ginger, peeled and chopped

1⅔ cups coconut milk

10½ ounces sweet potatoes, peeled and chopped
   into small cubes

1 (14½-ounce) can diced tomatoes

⅔ cup vegetable stock

3 tablespoons chopped cilantro leaves

2 tablespoons whole almonds

Sea salt and freshly ground black pepper

1 Cover the split peas with cold water and let soak overnight. The following morning, drain, rinse, and then set aside.

2 In a deep casserole dish, heat the olive oil, add the onion, and sauté over medium heat until it begins to caramelize, a few minutes. Add the crushed red pepper, garam masala, turmeric, cumin, and chopped ginger to the pot and cook for another minute to soften the ginger.

3 Add the coconut milk, split peas, diced sweet potatoes, diced tomatoes, and vegetable stock. Season well, cover, and simmer until the dhal is deliciously thick and the lentils are falling apart, about 1 hour. Top up with more hot stock if you think the dahl is becoming dry. Serve with the chopped cilantro and whole almonds.

SLOW-BAKED POTATO DAUPHINOISE

PREP TIME 15 MINUTES • COOK TIME 3 HOURS

The name "dauphinoise" originates from the Dauphine area of France. It is a mere coincidence that this regal dish is similar to "dauphin," the name bestowed upon the heir to the French throne. With all this history, it seems fitting that I would describe it as my "King of Sides." Cream, potato, and garlic, all baked very slowly, then ripening until the top is crowned with gold. Long live the monarchy!

SERVES 8

Butter, for greasing

1¼ cups heavy cream

1¼ cups crème fraîche (not lowfat, as this will split during cooking)

⅓ cup plus 1 tablespoon lowfat milk

3 large garlic cloves, peeled and crushed

1 onion, thinly sliced into rings

2¼ pounds mealy potatoes, peeled and sliced into ⅛-inch slices (or as near as you can get!)

Sea salt and freshly ground black pepper

1 Preheat your oven to 300°F and lightly grease a 2-quart ovenproof dish.

2 In a small pitcher, combine the cream, crème fraîche, milk, and garlic and let infuse for a few minutes.

3 Layer up the sliced potato and onion rings to cover the bottom of your dish. Season well, then continue to add layers until all the potato and onion slices have been used. Slowly pour over the creamy mixture, allowing each addition to find the crevices and disappear before adding more. Season again.

4 Bake in the oven for 3 hours.

A SIDE OF SPICED SWEET POTATO & PARSNIPS

PREP TIME 30 MINUTES • COOK TIME 45 MINUTES

If this recipe were to be featured in a lonely-hearts column, the entry might look something like this: "A plain vegetable seeks a vibrant fish to add interest to his relationship; despite dressing simply and despite much of life spent underground, he is willing to be served hot." Don't let the appearances of these two root vegetables put you off. A sprinkling of red pepper, garlic, and rosemary and a viciously hot oven will transform them and they will be perfect with any roast you cook.

PLENTY FOR 6

1 teaspoon cayenne pepper

1½ pounds sweet potatoes, scrubbed

1½ pounds parsnips, scrubbed and sliced into quarters lengthwise

½ teaspoon crushed red pepper

6 garlic cloves, bashed but not peeled

3 sprigs of rosemary

2 tablespoons olive oil

Sea salt and freshly ground black pepper

1 Preheat the oven to 400°F.

2 Place all the ingredients in a roasting pan and mix. Don't be afraid to get your hands involved, as you'll achieve the best coating that way. Season well.

3 Roast for 45 minutes, turning halfway through.

CREAMY ROASTED LEEK
& CAULIFLOWER

Cauliflower, with its mild and homey sort of flavor, is not one to steal the spotlight on a menu, but can be relied upon if it's given a moment's thought. I ate my fair share of cauliflower cheese throughout my childhood but feel that it deserves a makcover, and I'd argue this recipe is easier. It may take longer in the oven, but with no white sauce to contend with it is quick, simple, and exquisitely tasty.

PREP TIME 10 MINUTES　　　　**SERVES 6 (SIDE) OR 4 (MAIN)**　　　　COOK TIME 1 HOUR

1 (1¾-pound) cauliflower, divided into small florets about the size of a table tennis ball

2 medium leeks, cut in half lengthwise and then into ½- to ¾-inch crescents

½ teaspoon cumin seed (optional)

2 to 3 tablespoons oil

⅓ cup crème fraîche

⅔ cup heavy cream

2 teaspoons Dijon mustard

1 heaping cup shredded sharp cheddar cheese

Sea salt and freshly ground black pepper

1 Preheat the oven to 400°F. The key to this recipe is that the oven is hot, so if you're not completely confident your oven reaches that temperature, crank it up a notch and keep a watchful eye on the dish!

2 Put the cauliflower, leeks, and cumin seed into a large metal roasting pan. Coat with oil and give the whole thing a good jumble. Cover tightly with foil and roast in the hot oven for 40 minutes.

3 Take out of the oven and remove the foil; the leeks will have wilted and the cauliflower will be soft and steamy. Give everything a good stir.

4 Reduce the oven temperature to 350°F. Spoon over the crème fraîche, cream, and mustard and a healthy grinding of salt and pepper. Using a big spoon, mix everything together so it looks like a snowy mountain range. Sprinkle over the cheese, then bake for another 20 minutes until the top is perfectly golden.

HOLLOWED SQUASH
WITH LENTILS, ZUCCHINI & BLUE CHEESE

While I was living in Zimbabwe, butternut squash became as familiar a staple as bread and butter. We'd roast it, blitz it, make chocolate brownies from it… but there was always one winner and that was to stuff it. Like the African lifestyle, this recipe is happy to sit and chill for a little while once it escapes from the oven, making it perfect for entertaining. The recipe has a two-step process, so is perfect for making a day or two in advance.

PREP TIME 30 MINUTES — SERVES 4 — COOK TIME 30 MINUTES

1 large butternut squash
1 small zucchini
5 tablespoons crème fraîche
1 heaping cup crumbled Stilton or other blue cheese

1 (14- to 15-ounce) can green lentils, drained
1 tablespoon chopped flat-leaf parsley
Sea salt and freshly ground black pepper

1 Preheat the oven to 350°F.

2 Cut the butternut squash in half lengthwise and scoop out the seeds and discard. Place, flesh-side down, on an oiled baking sheet and bake for 30 minutes.

3 Meanwhile, prepare the filling. Slice the zucchini in half lengthwise and then chop into ¼-inch crescents. Place in a bowl with the crème fraîche, ⅔ cup of the blue cheese, the lentils, and parsley. Season, season, season. Cover and place in the fridge until needed.

4 Remove the squash from the oven—the flesh should be softening slightly but still have a bit of bite to it. Let stand for a few minutes until cool enough to the touch, then use a spoon to gently remove the flesh from the center of the squash. Don't veer too near the sides—allow ½ to ¾ inch around the edge—as you don't want the squash to collapse. Dice the flesh and add to the chilled mixture. (Stop here if preparing the dish in advance.)

5 Spoon the zucchini-and-squash loveliness into the hollowed-out squash halves. Keep on piling it in, pushing it down, and piling it in: it will fit, I'm sure of it. Finish by sprinkling the remaining cheese over the top and return to the oven to bake for another 30 minutes.

6 I suggest you let the squash halves sit for 10 minutes or so when they come out of the oven, as this allows the delicious liquid to be soaked up by the vegetables.

EGGPLANT RACKS
WITH HALLOUMI, LEMON & THYME

In my humble opinion, eggplants get a raw deal—they are known for nothing more than Greek mousaka and Turkish baba ganoush, but I believe the silky purple orbs should be treated with respect. Here is a creative way of cooking eggplants that takes no time to prepare and lets the oven (or fire) do its work. Serve for lunch with a simple pile of dressed arugula.

PREP TIME 10 MINUTES
PLUS 1 HOUR MARINATING

SERVES 3 TO 4 AS A SIDE

COOK TIME 1 HOUR

2 large eggplants

Juice of 1 large lemon

2 tablespoons extra virgin olive oil

½ red onion, sliced into thin rings

4½ ounces halloumi cheese, sliced into ¼- to ½-inch slices

1 small red chile, seeded and finely chopped

8 sprigs of thyme

Freshly ground black pepper

1 Place each eggplant in turn on a cutting board and allow it to fall on its side. Gently slice vertically at ⅝-inch intervals, cutting deep into the flesh but taking care not to slice all the way through to the bottom.

2 Sprinkle the lemon juice and olive oil all over the eggplants, making sure they drizzle into the cracks. Leave for an hour or so to ensure the flesh soaks up all those beautiful flavors.

3 Preheat the oven to 400°F.

4 When you are ready, stuff the onion rings and halloumi into alternate slits in the eggplants as if you're putting toast in a toast rack. Don't worry if they poke above the eggplant—it will sort itself out in the oven. Scatter over the red chile, squeeze the thyme sprigs among the racks, and give them a good grinding of black pepper.

5 Place the eggplant on oiled foil and enclose in a packet shape. Bake in the oven for 45 minutes. Open the packet and roast for another 15 minutes.

 TIP—THE MARINATING TIME IN THIS RECIPE IS IMPORTANT, AS IT BEGINS TO BREAK DOWN THE EGGPLANT FLESH. DON'T BE TEMPTED TO DO LESS THAN AN HOUR, BUT OF COURSE YOU COULD LEAVE THEM OVERNIGHT IF IT HELPS EASE PREPARATIONS ON THE DAY.

OEUFS EN COCOTTE WITH SORREL & GARLIC

PREP TIME 5 MINUTES • COOK TIME 20 MINUTES

"Baked eggs" might be a more familiar title for this recipe, but I think the French translation reads more romantically, as it so often does. Just five ingredients sit together flawlessly and require but a moment's preparation—a lemony edge of sorrel and a kick of garlic cut through the delicate egg and cream, making for a yummy, very miniature one pot.

SERVES 4

Butter, for greasing

A handful of fresh sorrel, coarsely chopped (or replace with wilted spinach and the zest of 1 lemon)

4 tablespoons heavy cream

1 garlic clove, peeled and very well crushed

4 large free-range eggs

A few sprigs of dill weed or chervil

Sea salt and freshly ground black pepper

1 Preheat the oven to 350°F. Lightly grease the inside of 4 (9-ounce) ramekins.

2 In a small pitcher, lightly beat together the sorrel, cream, and garlic and season with sea salt flakes and plenty of black pepper. Pour your mixture into the ramekins and crack an egg on top of each. Garnish with dill weed or chervil.

3 Place the ramekins in a roasting pan, then pour enough boiling water into the pan to reach halfway up the ramekins—this creates a lovely, steamy environment for the eggs so there is no chance of them drying out. Carefully transfer to the oven and cook for 15 to 20 minutes.

4 Serve with a good grinding of black pepper.

QUICHE IN A SUITCASE

PREP TIME 15 MINUTES • COOK TIME 1 HOUR

One of my oldest friends, Jenny, lives near Borough Market in London, just close enough to smell the charred chorizo and indulge in a roast pork roll more often than necessary. During one morning spent there I talked to a baker about the possibility of making a quiche within a hollowed loaf, rather than pie dough. Could it be done? Yes it can.

SERVES 8

1 large boule of bread, approx. 10-inch round and 1¾ pounds in weight

6 medium free-range eggs

1¼ cups heavy cream

1 heaping cup shredded sharp cheddar cheese

1⅔ cups cherry tomatoes, halved horizontally

2 cups coarsely chopped basil

Sea salt and freshly ground black pepper

1 Preheat the oven to 325°F. Cut about a third off the top of the loaf of bread to give a depth of 2½ to 3¼ inches for the filling. Hollow out the inside by removing 90 percent of the crumb, but be careful not to make the shell too thin or it might not stand up to the filling; about ½ inch thick is perfect. (Now what could you do with the inside? Bread sauce, croutons, or see page 33 for a quick panzanella.)

2 Crack the eggs into a medium-size bowl and lightly beat with a fork. Then simply pour in the cream and add two-thirds each of the cheddar, tomatoes, and basil. Season heavily.

3 Pour into your suitcase. There should be about a 1-inch clearance from the top of the mixture to the lip of the bread. Dress the top of the mixture with the remaining cheese, tomatoes, and basil. Give a good grinding of black pepper and bake for 1 hour, or until the filling is firm to the touch. Turn off the oven and let the quiche cool inside. To serve, simply slice into wedges.

FISH FOOD

Not long ago, I spent a sunny day surfing off the coast of Cornwall, South West England. We lay lethargically sunbathing on boards, limbs dangling, hopeful that the unobliging sea would cough up some waves or at least entertainment. Then I started to get nervous. My mother is right; why does one don fancy dress, willingly lie in deep water disguised as seals, and wait to be attacked? Perhaps it's natural, but I do find all of those fishes, mollusks, unknown and undiscovered things that reside in water quite intimidating.

The same could be said of a fish counter. We go back, time after time, like bees to a honeypot, choosing the same old fish, never venturing near an unfamiliar shape or odd-looking flat fish. A little bit of knowhow and these fish seem far more approachable, so I hope you might take a few minutes to choose a recipe that takes you a small step away from your comfort zone. You never know, you may just surprise yourself.

STEAMED SALMON
ON A BED OF BEANS, CHILE & ZUCCHINI

When a chef declares that the main dish has been cooked *en papillotte*, you may think that he or she is worthy of admiration. But for those in the know, this culinary technique is as simple as wrapping a gift. It merely means creating a packet that speedily steams the food—generally fish, fruit, or vegetables—and seals in the flavors. All that the guests have to do is unwrap their gift.

PREP TIME 10 MINUTES · SERVES 2 · COOK TIME 25 MINUTES

1 (15-ounce) can kidney beans, drained and rinsed

1 small zucchini, grated

3 garlic cloves, peeled and finely chopped

2 red chiles, seeded and finely chopped (reserve a bit for garnish)

½ teaspoon nigella (black onion) seed, plus extra for sprinkling

Grated zest and juice of 1 lemon

1 tablespoon chervil leaves (use dill weed if you can't find any chervil), plus extra for garnish

2 teaspoons Dijon mustard

2 salmon fillets, skinned

2 teaspoons butter

2 tablespoons dry white wine

Sea salt and freshly ground black pepper

1 Preheat the oven to 375°F.

2 In a bowl, combine the kidney beans, zucchini, garlic, chiles, nigella seed, lemon zest and juice, chervil (or dill weed), and mustard, giving everything a good jumble. Season this mixture well.

3 Lay two lengths of parchment paper or foil, about 14 inches long, on your work surface. Split the vegetable mixture in half and spoon on top of each piece of foil. Nestle a salmon fillet in the center, season, and then top with the butter, a sprinkling of nigella seed, and a scattering of chervil.

4 Seal the sides of the packet, leaving a small gap to pour 1 tablespoon of wine into each, then seal completely. Make sure there aren't any holes, as it's the contained steam that will cook the contents—if there is an accidental tear, wrap with another piece of parchment paper/foil.

5 Pop in the oven for 25 minutes. Tear open the packet and serve with the rest of the bottle of wine. Idyllic.

BAKED WHOLE SEA BASS
WITH EGGPLANT & TAMARIND

Some recipes can't be bracketed into particular continents. As Anna Hansen—chef at the Modern Pantry in London—believes, ingredients aren't specific to certain countries, "they are simply a worldwide larder." Here, we have a Thai–Indian recipe that is stuffed with big, global flavors. It's a no-fuss way of cooking fish that makes for a wonderfully rustic meal.

PREP TIME 20 MINUTES   SERVES 4 TO 6   COOK TIME 35 MINUTES

3 tablespoons olive oil

3 small onions, thinly sliced

1 large eggplant, cut into 1¼-inch cubes

3 garlic cloves, peeled and thinly sliced

½ tablespoon curry powder

1¼-inch chunk of fresh ginger, peeled and grated

½ tablespoon jarred tamarind concentrate, mixed with
  2 tablespoons boiling water

2 hot red chiles (or as many or as few as you wish),
  cut into chunky diagonals

6 medium tomatoes, cut into quarters

1¼ cups coconut milk

4 small sea bass, scaled and gutted, the heads removed

Cilantro, chopped

Sea salt and freshly ground black pepper

1 Preheat the oven to 400°F. In a large ovenproof pot, heat 2 tablespoons of the olive oil over medium heat. Add the onions and eggplant and let sizzle until the eggplant begins to break down and look a bit charred, about 8 minutes.

2 Add the garlic, curry powder, and ginger and cook for another minute. The pot should smell delicious. Now, simply stir through the tamarind, chiles, tomato quarters, and coconut milk, then remove from the heat.

3 Slash the fish three times on the diagonal on both sides and season well, not forgetting the cavity.

4 Snuggle the fish on top of your curry bed. (You could transfer to a roasting pan here if your initial pot isn't quite long enough.) Season again. Drizzle with the remaining oil and roast, uncovered, in the oven for 20 to 25 minutes. The flesh should be firm and crispy and the vegetables saucy and broken down.

5 Using a spatula, remove the fish and, holding a sharp knife flat against the back bone, fillet each one.

6 Serve a pile of juicy vegetables with a fillet of sea bass alongside. Scatter with chopped cilantro to finish off the plate beautifully.

 TIP—IF YOU DON'T FEEL CONFIDENT FILLETING FISH ONCE IT'S COOKED, SIMPLY BUY SEA BASS FILLETS AND COOK THE VEGETABLES ALONE IN THE OVEN FOR 15 MINUTES, BEFORE ADDING THE FILLETS FOR ANOTHER 10 MINUTES.

WHITING, LIMA BEAN
& RED BELL PEPPER STEW

We are rapidly running out of our favorite fish. They have quite simply been eaten out of house and sea, and as loyal fish eaters it is time we gave the cods, tunas, and salmons a chance to regroup and rebreed. Whiting can be just as plump as its cousinly cod and has a wonderfully delicate flavor, which will balance with the sweet red bell peppers.

PREP TIME 20 MINUTES   SERVES 4 TO 6   COOK TIME 35 MINUTES

2 tablespoons olive oil

10½ ounces shallots, finely sliced

2 red bell peppers, sliced into ½- to ¾-inch lengths

3 garlic cloves, peeled and thinly sliced

1 teaspoon Spanish smoked paprika

¾ cup dry white wine

2 (15-ounce) cans lima beans, rinsed and drained

Grated zest and juice of 1 lemon

3 tablespoons crème fraîche

½ cup pitted black olives

18 ounces whiting fillet, cut into chunks

2 tablespoons coarsely chopped cilantro

1 In a 2-quart pot, heat the olive oil over low heat. Add the shallots, red bell peppers, garlic, and paprika and cook gently, covered, until the vegetables soften. This needs to be a gentle process—try not to get any color on the shallots—and can take a while, about 15 minutes.

2 Pour in the wine, turn up the heat, and bring to a boil to allow the alcohol to burn off and the liquid to reduce by half. Add the beans and lemon zest and juice to the pot. Cook through for a couple of minutes before returning to low heat. Stir through the crème fraîche and olives and warm through.

3 Gently place the whiting on top of the stew and cover with a lid. Steam over low heat until the fish is translucent and opaque all the way through, 10 to 12 minutes. Remove the lid, turn off the heat, and sprinkle over the cilantro. Serve before the fish has any chance to overcook.

CARAMELIZED FISH POT

This pot is inspired by fond memories of being engulfed by the sweet caramel aroma that lingers like fog in cities throughout Vietnam. On any visit, you'll notice caramel sauce is widely used in the country's cooking for braising to provide both an intense flavor and a deliciously glazed appearance to the finished food. Catfish is the traditional fish of choice for a fish pot, as the flesh is very meaty, but halibut is a good alternative and may well be easier to find.

PREP TIME 15 MINUTES · SERVES 4 · COOK TIME 20 MINUTES

4 meaty white fish steaks (approx. 1¼ pounds total weight), e.g. halibut, catfish, or whiting

2 tablespoons fish sauce

3 tablespoons peanut or sesame oil

⅓ cup superfine sugar

3½ ounces shallots, finely chopped

2 garlic cloves, peeled and sliced

2-inch piece of fresh ginger, peeled and finely chopped

½ cup coconut juice

1 fiery red chile, seeded and finely chopped

3 to 4 scallions, chopped

Sea salt and freshly ground black pepper

TO SERVE

Steamed rice

A good handful of Vietnamese mint

Lime wedges

1 In a bowl, marinate the fish in the fish sauce and just 1 tablespoon of the peanut or sesame oil while you start making the caramel sauce.

2 In a heavy-bottom iron pot—or, if you are lucky enough to own a clay pot, this is the moment to get it out!— heat the remaining oil. Add the sugar and stir to combine. Keep the heat high and let the mixture caramelize. This can take some minutes, so be patient, stirring only every 30 seconds or so.

3 Once you have a lovely caramel emerging, throw in the shallots, garlic, and ginger. Stir so they are completely coated before pouring in the coconut juice. Be careful: your pot will spit like an angry dragon. Some lumps of sugar may appear because the juice is cold, but continue to heat, stirring, until they disappear.

4 Add the marinated fish and chopped chile and reduce the heat to medium/low. Cover with a lid and let the fish steam for 10 to 12 minutes.

5 Remove from the heat, adjust the seasoning, adding a little more fish sauce if you fancy, and stir through the scallions. Serve in small bowls with the steamed rice, mint, and a lime wedge or two.

 TIP—THIS POT IS PREDOMINANTLY FISH AND IN ORDER TO BULK IT OUT A BIT I SUGGEST SERVING IT WITH SOME STEAMED RICE—A CARBOHYDRATE ACCOMPANIMENT WILL MAKE YOUR FISH STRETCH FAR MORE.

STUFFED MACKEREL
CURLS WITH CRUNCHY POTATOES

I think this recipe is incredible, with mackerel fillets transformed from quite a frugal understudy of an ingredient to the sophisticated star of the show. The end result is wonderfully healthy in an Italian sort of way, with plenty of olive oil, garlic, lemon, and seasoning. Many a time we've enjoyed the leftovers a day afterward, cold and bleached with purple, straight from a Tupperware dish in the fridge.

PREP TIME 20 MINUTES   SERVES 6   COOK TIME 45 MINUTES

3 tablespoons extra virgin olive oil, plus extra for greasing

1¾ pounds new potatoes, scrubbed clean and cut into large chunks

1 head of garlic divided into cloves, the outer paper on each clove kept intact

9 ounces cooked beets, grated (and any excess liquid squeezed away)

2¼ cups fresh, fluffy white bread crumbs

A (¾-ounce) bunch of dill weed, coarsely chopped

Grated zest and juice of 1 large lemon

6 mackerel fillets, skin on but pin-boned

Sea salt and freshly ground black pepper

½ cup thick plain yogurt, to serve

You will also need 6 wooden toothpicks

1 Preheat the oven to 400°F.

2 Rub a large roasting pan with a bit of oil to prevent any sticking. Throw in the potatoes and whole garlic cloves, drizzle with 2 tablespoons of the oil, and season. Give the whole pan a good shake. Roast in the hot oven for 30 minutes, turning halfway through to make sure the bottoms aren't catching.

3 Meanwhile, make the stuffing: in a small bowl, combine the grated beets, bread crumbs, half the chopped dill weed, and the lemon zest and season well. Mix until the consistency is pliable and holds its shape—you could squeeze a little lemon juice in if it needs to be slightly more moist.

4 Lie the mackerel fillets on a board and top each one with a good spoonful of stuffing. Fold the fillet in half lengthwise to encase the stuffing and secure with a toothpick. Don't worry if you have any leftover stuffing—it can just be spooned over the potatoes.

5 Remove the potatoes from the oven and rest the six stuffed fillets on top. Spoon any leftover stuffing around the fillets and drizzle with the remaining olive oil. Roast for 12 to 15 minutes, or until the fish feels firm to the touch. Serve with a good spoonful of thick yogurt and the remaining dill weed.

BAKED FINNAN HADDIE
WITH GNOCCHI & GREENS

Finnan haddie (smoked haddock) has a gutsy character, pushing it to prominence in any dish it chooses to star in. Here, pillows of gnocchi and delicate green vegetables act as supporting roles in a dish that might just become your "new fish pie."

PREP TIME 10 MINUTES	SERVES 3 TO 4	COOK TIME 35 MINUTES

18 ounces fresh gnocchi

7 ounces baby zucchini, sliced at an angle into
¼-inch rounds, or 2 small zucchini, halved down
the center and chopped into crescents

9 ounces asparagus, cut into ¾-inch lengths

¾ cup plus 1 tablespoon crème fraîche

1 tablespoon finely chopped dill weed

¾ pound finnan haddie (smoked haddock), skinned
and cut into 1-inch pieces

4 tablespoons grated Parmesan cheese

Sea salt and freshly ground black pepper

1 One piece of advice: get everything ready beforehand because, once you get going, this can be quite a quick recipe! Make sure you have a large, shallow pot that can go both on the stovetop and in the oven.

2 Preheat the oven to 400°F.

3 Fill your pot with water and place on high heat. Bring to a boil and add the gnocchi, zucchini, and asparagus. Cook for 3 minutes, no more and no less, then drain.

4 Return the cooked gnocchi and vegetables to the pot and stir in the crème fraîche and dill weed. Next, a little more gently, add the pieces of fish. Mix until all the ingredients are evenly distributed and then give the dish a good season with black pepper and a little salt.

5 Scatter with the Parmesan and cook, covered, in the oven for 15 to 20 minutes, until the vegetables have softened but still retain a little bite. That's it... now you can put your feet up while your pot is happily cooking.

 TIP—A WORD OF WARNING: DON'T USE LOWFAT CRÈME FRAÎCHE, AS SADLY IT WILL SPLIT DURING COOKING.

RICE NOODLE
SHRIMP & FRESH HERB SALAD

This recipe seems just so healthful. I think perhaps it's the pure, glassy appearance of the rice noodles and the lack of gluten that stops them congregating, pasta-style, in your stomach for hours after eating. Enjoyed all over East Asia and added as a staple to broths and stir-fries, they are my noodle of choice. The recipe does require quite a lot of chopping, but with a sharp knife you'll cut through it in no time. Putting it all together at the end is a cinch.

PREP TIME 15 MINUTES   SERVES 4   COOK TIME 2 MINUTES

5½ ounces dry vermicelli rice noodles

A drizzle of mild olive oil

10½ ounces large cooked and peeled shrimp

1 green apple, cored and sliced paper thin

6 ounces sugar snap peas, each cut into 3 on the diagonal

3 tablespoons chopped mint

Heaping ⅓ cup coarsely chopped dry-roasted peanuts

3 tablespoons chopped cilantro or Thai basil, plus
   a little extra to garnish

Juice of 2 limes

2 tablespoons fish sauce

1 teaspoon superfine sugar

1 Dunk the noodles into a pan full of boiling water and cook for 1½ minutes so they have softened but not overcooked—they will continue to soften once they are in the salad. Drain and cool under cold running water. Transfer to a large bowl and drizzle over a little olive oil to stop the strands sticking together.

2 Here is the easy bit: simply add all of the other ingredients (holding back a cluster of peanuts), and combine so everything is evenly distributed. Serve right away with the reserved peanuts and extra chopped cilantro or Thai basil resting on top.

DRUNKEN MUSSELS
WITH HARD CIDER, LEEKS & CHORIZO

There is something satisfying about discovering a blanket of mussels clinging to a rock, plucking them from their home and then dropping them in the sink to take a bath—though, of course, the supermarket is an easier way to acquire the shellfish! Mussels are at their juiciest during the first and last three months of the year, so pick your moment, savor the preparation, and inhale the sea steam as the cooking begins.

PREP TIME 20 MINUTES	SERVES 2	COOK TIME 15 MINUTES

18 ounces live, fresh mussels

2 tablespoons mild olive oil

2 tablespoons (¼ stick) butter

3½ ounces cooking chorizo, sliced into thin rounds

2 garlic cloves, peeled and finely chopped

2 medium leeks, finely sliced into rounds

A cluster of thyme sprigs

1⅔ cups hard cider

3 tablespoons heavy cream

Plenty of freshly chopped flat-leaf parsley

Bread, to serve

1 First prepare the mussels. Scrub them to remove any sand or beards, knocking away any barnacles if you discover them. Discard any open mussels that refuse to close even when given a sharp tap. Rinse well under cold water and set aside.

2 In a large saucepan, heat the olive oil and butter over medium heat. Add the chorizo and sauté for a few minutes until you have a rust-colored bubbling larva at the bottom of the pot. Add the garlic, leeks, and thyme and cook until the leeks begin to soften and lose their shape, a few minutes more.

3 Turn up the heat and add the hard cider and mussels. Cover tightly with a lid and steam for 5 to 7 minutes, shaking the pan once or twice to encourage the mussels to open. Reduce the heat to a simmer and, using a large slotted spoon, remove the mussels to deep warmed bowls, again discarding any that have not opened.

4 Pour the cream into the juices and cook for another couple of minutes before dredging your waiting mussels. Sprinkle parsley liberally on top and serve with a chunk of bread to mop up the juices.

TOMATO, ANCHOVY
& GARLIC ANGEL HAIR PASTA

Most of us have been victims of "summer jobs" in school vacations. My pennies (literally) were earned tending to the neighbors' dogs, vegetables, or mail while they were on vacation. One occupation that cropped up many times over was looking after Mr. Pask's tomatoes. He had a tiny greenhouse that became stiflingly sweaty in the summer sun and was packed with tomato plants dripping with fruit. Years later I only think a tomato is really good if it smells like that greenhouse, dusty with scent, and is deep red in color.

PREP TIME 15 MINUTES · SERVES 4 · COOK TIME 20 MINUTES

4 tablespoons olive oil

4 large garlic cloves, peeled and finely chopped

1 teaspoon crushed red pepper

1½ pounds fresh tomatoes, coarsely chopped

2 cups hot vegetable stock

14 ounces dry angel hair pasta

4½ ounces fresh anchovy fillets in olive oil, drained and coarsely chopped, or kept whole if you prefer

A handful of basil leaves, coarsely chopped (reserve a few whole leaves for garnish)

Sea salt and freshly ground black pepper

1 In a large, deep saucepan, heat the oil over medium heat. Add the garlic and crushed red pepper and cook until the smell is released, about 1 minute.

2 Add the chopped tomatoes (stand back to avoid the spitting!) and turn the heat down to low. Cook, covered, for 8 to 10 minutes, stirring halfway through. By this stage almost all the tomatoes should have broken down. Season with a generous pinch of salt and plenty of freshly ground black pepper.

3 Pour the vegetable stock into the pan, bring to a simmer, then reduce the heat to low. Add the pasta and cook, covered, for 5 to 6 minutes, giving everything a good stir halfway through.

4 Stir in three-quarters of the anchovy fillets and the chopped basil until all is beautifully combined. You should add a touch more stock here if you feel it's needed.

5 Serve immediately, with a basil leaf and the remaining anchovies balancing on top.

SHRIMP, ARTICHOKE
& LEMON RISOTTO

One bag of risotto rice can rescue you from many a tricky culinary situation: it can become a creamy rice dessert to be eaten with an immense spoonful of homemade strawberry jam, risotto cakes branded crispy from a second pan-frying, or, as here, it can be cooked with garlic, hot stock, and punchy ingredients. The three keys to a risotto's success are: a chef with the patience of a bird watcher, ingredients that scream quality, and guests who are ready! Unlike bird watchers, risotto is decidedly impatient and doesn't like to be kept waiting.

PREP TIME 10 MINUTES   SERVES 4   COOK TIME 25 MINUTES

2 tablespoons olive oil

1 onion, finely chopped

2 garlic cloves, peeled and finely chopped

½ teaspoon fennel seed

1¾ cups dry Arborio or Carnaroli risotto rice

¾ cup dry white wine

About 5 cups piping-hot vegetable stock

9 ounces raw jumbo shrimp, peeled and deveined but with the tails still attached

Grated zest and juice of 1 lemon

8 marinated artichoke hearts, drained and quartered

4 tablespoons finely grated Parmesan cheese, plus extra to serve

Sea salt and freshly ground black pepper

TO SERVE

Sprigs of fresh dill weed

A drizzle of extra virgin olive oil

1 In a deep sauté pan, heat the olive oil over low heat. Add the onion and sauté until it is soft but not colored, about 5 minutes. Add the garlic and fennel seed and continue to cook for 1 minute more.

2 Over gentle heat, add the risotto rice to the pan and stir so the grains are coated in oil. Add the white wine and stir until absorbed. Gradually add the stock, one ladleful at a time, stirring each one until it's absorbed before adding the next. The amount of stock you add should become smaller when the rice is nearly done—this is a delicate process! Season.

3 When the risotto is al dente and the pan isn't dry, add the shrimp and the lemon zest and juice. Cook until the shrimp have turned a rosy-cheek pink, 2 to 3 minutes. Have a taste and see if the seasoning is correct—if not, this is your moment. Stir in the artichoke hearts and Parmesan until warmed through.

4 Finally, make sure the consistency is correct: risotto shouldn't hold its shape; instead it should slowly crawl to the edge of the plate on which it is served. Add a little more hot stock if you think the finished dish could be a little looser. Serve with a sprig of fresh dill weed and a drizzle of olive oil, plus some extra Parmesan for the table.

SLOW-COOKED SQUID
WITH CHORIZO & BEANS

Flash-frying squid may be the most familiar method of cooking this ocean delicacy, but here is a slow-cooked alternative. The squid seemingly tenses after initial cooking, though quickly relaxes into the pot after a longer soak in its bathtub of wine. A mellow flavor complements the fiery chorizo and herbed, juicy beans that I hope you will enjoy.

PREP TIME 15 MINUTES   SERVES 4   COOK TIME 1 HOUR

1 tablespoon olive oil

5½ ounces cooking chorizo, cut into ½-inch rounds

1 large red onion, finely sliced

3 garlic cloves, peeled and finely chopped

1 large red chile, seeded and finely sliced

2 large plum tomatoes, each cut into 8 wedges

¾ cup sweet white wine

⅔ cup hot chicken stock

1 bouquet garni, made up of 2 fresh bay leaves, 2 to 3 flat-leaf parsley stems (reserve the leaves for the garnish), and a cluster of fresh thyme

14 ounces cleaned squid tubes, sliced into ½-inch rings (keep the tentacles if you are able)

1 (14-ounce) can flageolet beans, drained and rinsed

Sea salt and freshly ground black pepper

1 In a large casserole dish, heat the oil over high heat. Add the chorizo and pan-fry until it begins to crisp, has colored at the edges, and has filled the kitchen with its scent.

2 Remove the chorizo from the pan using a slotted spoon and add the onion to the oil left behind. Reduce the heat to medium and sauté the onion for a couple of minutes before adding the garlic and chile. Continue to cook for until both the onion and garlic are soft, 2 to 3 minutes.

3 Stir through the tomato wedges and cook until they have begun to loose their shape, about 2 minutes. Pour in the white wine and reduce by half, allowing the alcohol to boil off.

4 Stir in the stock, then return the chorizo to the pot along with the bouquet garni and the squid rings. Simmer gently, covered, for 30 minutes. Add the beans and cook, uncovered, for a final 20 minutes.

5 Serve garnished with the reserved parsley leaves and a good grinding of salt and pepper.

FISH BROTH
WITH NEW POTATOES & FRESH GREEN PESTO

"You are what you eat" is a mantra we've all grown familiar with and I agree that cleansing food makes for a cleansed mind. This particular recipe, with its fresh fish poached in a wonderful hot broth, makes me feel virtuous whether I've run a "10K" or sat through a TV marathon. As is often the case, don't add the fish until the last possible moment to avoid overcooking it.

PREP TIME 15 MINUTES   SERVES 4   COOK TIME 25 MINUTES

2 red snapper fillets, skin on, cut into 1½- to
   2-inch pieces
8 raw jumbo shrimp, peeled and deveined but
   with the tails still attached
7 ounces white fish fillet (flounder or fluke), cut into
   1½- to 2-inch pieces
12 live, fresh mussels, beards removed and scrubbed
8 clams, scrubbed
2 teaspoons olive oil

1 large onion, chopped
2 garlic cloves, peeled and finely chopped
1¼ pounds new potatoes, scrubbed, larger ones halved
⅓ cup good-quality fresh green pesto
1 cup sweet white wine
1 quart hot fish stock
3 plum tomatoes, coarsely diced
1¾ cups coarsely chopped watercress
Crusty loaf, to serve

1 Prepare your fish and have it sitting calmly on a plate in the fridge ready for the final step. The minutes pass more quickly than you think and it's good to be prepared.

2 In a large saucepan, heat the oil over medium heat. Add the onion and sauté until it begins to soften, about 2 minutes, then add the garlic. Continue to sauté until the onion has cooked, but be careful not to let it color.

3 Add the potatoes and pesto and stir to combine. Pour over the white wine and fish stock and bring to a boil.

Reduce the heat and simmer until the potatoes are almost tender, about 15 minutes. Add the tomatoes and continue to simmer for 5 minutes. (Pop some bread in the oven so you can serve the fish with a warm, crusty loaf.)

4 This is the last step and should be done when your guests are already sitting at the table. Add the fish, shellfish, and watercress to the pot and cook, covered, until the mussels and clams have opened and the fish has turned opaque, 2 to 3 minutes. Ladle into bowls and serve immediately. Don't let that fish overcook!

 TIP—I'D RECOMMEND HAVING A LARGE BOWL OF WARM WATER ON THE TABLE WITH A SLICE OF LEMON OR TWO. THAT WAY YOUR GUESTS CAN RINSE THEIR FINGERS AFTER REMOVING THE SHRIMP TAILS AND MUSSEL SHELLS.

ALL-IN-ONE FISH PIE

Fish pie is the edible equivalent of a robust bear hug, but oh my, making the traditional dish is a little more time consuming. However, this one-pot fish pie has had a makeover. It relies on a few minor tweaks and tricks, making it absolutely scrumptious, ready within the hour, and with minimal cleanup.

PREP TIME 15 MINUTES **SERVES 6** COOK TIME 30 MINUTES

Olive oil, for greasing

9 ounces pollock fillets, skinned and cut into delicate ¾- to 1¼-inch chunks

9 ounces salmon, skinned and cut into delicate ¾- to 1¼-inch chunks

9 ounces finnan haddie (smoked haddock), skinned and cut into delicate ¾- to 1¼-inch chunks

2 tablespoons all-purpose flour

1 red onion, very finely sliced

2 carrots (approx. 7 ounces), peeled and coarsely grated

1 cup frozen green peas (no need to precook them)

2 cups good-quality, store-bought white sauce, or homemade if you have the time

A good clump of dill weed, coarsely chopped

Grated zest of 1 lemon

5½ ounces phyllo dough sheets

4 tablespoons (½ stick) butter, melted

Sea salt and freshly ground black pepper

1 Preheat the oven to 350°F. Lightly grease a 1½- to 2-quart ovenproof dish with a little olive oil.

2 Put the fish chunks in a large bowl and sprinkle over the flour. Gently toss so each piece of fish is lightly coated. Add the vegetables, white sauce, dill weed (reserving a little for the garnish), and lemon zest. Gently combine so the sauce is spread throughout the mixture. Season and transfer to the ovenproof dish.

3 Brush one side of the phyllo dough sheets with butter and then scrunch up, leaving the buttered side facing upward. Place on top of the fish mixture. There is no need to be too neat; the more abstract, the more beautiful, in my opinion. Give a good twist of black pepper, a sprinkling of salt, and a little dusting of the reserved dill weed.

4 Bake in the oven for 30 to 35 minutes, until the phyllo is golden on top and the sauce is bubbling below. Remove from the oven and let stand to allow the fish to continue cooking for 5 minutes or so before serving.

 TIP—IF YOU HAVE A FEROCIOUS OVEN AND YOUR PHYLLO LOOKS TO BE BROWNING TOO QUICKLY, COVER WITH A PIECE OF FOIL FOR THE LAST FEW MINUTES OF COOKING.

CLUCKY & GAME

Winter 2011 was spent living in Zimbabwe on a chicken farm. I didn't visit the birds every day, but as I approached their houses, a musty, organic smell swept through the shiny wire and I was fully aware I'd left London smog behind.

Life for the chickens began in a hatchery where eggs were cautiously warmed and turned until the chicks were ready to fracture their fragile houses. The babies burst forth, tiny and bare-bodied, nobly fighting for survival to make it through their first hours. With every day the chicks grew stronger on our African soil, breathing in the sun, inhaling their feed, and scrabbling in red dust. My neighbors seemed happy.

Our house rations proffered three chickens a week, so it was during these months I became more speedy at jointing a chicken then ever before. We played with roasting, steaming, pot roasting, poaching, and frying. You name it, we tried it. Within this chapter are both chicken and game recipes that have been given a seal of approval and have been tested with both African and English meats.

CHICKEN & SAUSAGE
CASSOULET

Forget those canned concoctions of baked beans and rubbery frankfurters. Yes, the traditional French cassoulet does require some preparation, but once you're over the initial effort you can just sit back and let the flavors develop and mingle. It really is worth every minute. *Bon appétit.*

PREP TIME 1 HOUR (PLUS OVERNIGHT SOAKING)   **SERVES 8**   COOK TIME 2½ HOURS

2½ cups dry navy or cannellini beans

2 tablespoons olive oil

6 free-range chicken drumsticks, skin on

4 free-range chicken thighs, skin on

6 Toulouse sausages

7 ounces bacon, cut into dice

2 onions, cut in half

12 cloves

2 carrots, scrubbed clean and cut in half widthwise

4 garlic cloves, peeled and left whole

2 celery stalks, each sliced into 5

2 fresh bay leaves

4 to 5 sprigs of thyme

1 tablespoon tomato paste

Sea salt and freshly ground black pepper

1 The night before you want to cook, put the beans into a large bowl and cover with cold water. Let soak overnight, then drain and put in a large, heavy-bottom casserole dish with a capacity of about 6⅓ quarts. Cover the beans with fresh water and bring to a rolling boil for 10 minutes, then drain again and set the softened beans aside.

2 Heat the olive oil in the casserole and set about browning the chicken, sausage, and bacon. This will have to be done in batches so the meat browns rather than steams; the rule of thumb is that there should be ½ inch of space around each piece of meat. Cut the sausage in half, then cover all the meat and set aside.

3 Wipe the pot clean and add the soaked beans. Stud each onion half with 3 cloves and add them to the pot along with the carrots, garlic, celery, bay leaves, and a sprig or two of thyme. Top up with approximately 1½ quarts fresh water, then cover, bring to a simmer, and gently cook for an hour. The beans will still be quite firm at this stage.

4 Preheat the oven to 350°F.

5 Remove the studded onion halves and discard. Add the browned meat to the pot and gently stir in. Add the tomato paste and a few more thyme sprigs. Season the dish more than you think you need and pop it in the oven. Cook, covered, for 1½ hours. Check occasionally to make sure the cassoulet isn't drying out—add hot water if needed.

6 Remove any unwieldy thyme sprigs just before serving and give the whole thing a stir. You've done it and, my goodness, doesn't it smell good.

POT ROAST CHICKEN
WITH NEW POTATOES & SPINACH

A one-pot recipe book without a pot roast chicken would be like Thanksgiving without a turkey, and there's a reason why this recipe, in particular, became a staple Italian meal. Once you've made the stuffing it's a throw-it-all-in affair that can be a lifesaver when preparing a busy weekend lunch.

PREP TIME 20 MINUTES   **SERVES 6**   COOK TIME 1 HOUR 20 MINUTES

2¼ cups fresh, fine bread crumbs

2 garlic cloves, peeled and crushed

3 tablespoons good-quality basil pesto

½ nutmeg, grated, or 1 teaspoon ground nutmeg

3 tablespoons chopped flat-leaf parsley

1 free-range egg, beaten

1 whole (approx. 3-pound) free-range chicken

1 tablespoon vegetable oil

1 onion, cut into wedges

2 fresh bay leaves

3 celery stalks, cut into ¾-inch chunks

2¼ pounds baby new potatoes, scrubbed, large ones cut in half

1 quart hot chicken stock

1 (9-ounce) bag spinach

Sea salt and freshly ground black pepper

You will also need a 12-inch length of kitchen twine or a few wooden toothpicks.

1 Make the stuffing: in a bowl, mix together the bread crumbs, garlic, pesto, nutmeg, 2 tablespoons of the parsley, and the egg. Ram into the cavity of the chicken and, using the kitchen twine or toothpicks, do your best to close the opening completely.

2 Rub the chicken with salt and pepper. In a large casserole dish, heat the vegetable oil and, using tongs to help you, brown the chicken on all sides. As my mother would say, resist the urge to keep moving the chicken. Let each side brown before turning to another.

3 Turn down the heat. Add the onion wedges, bay leaves, celery, and potatoes around the chicken and pour in the stock. Bring the whole lot to a boil, cover, and reduce to a simmer until your chicken is cooked, about 1 hour—test that the juices run clear.

4 Take the chicken out of the pot (a word of warning… wear an apron to avoid being splattered) and set aside to cool slightly. Meanwhile, add the spinach and remaining parsley to the broth and let wilt. Squish the potatoes slightly if you would like the sauce to thicken up.

5 Cut the chicken into single servings (I find kitchen shears the best for this), then remove the stuffing and slice it into six. Spoon the vegetables into shallow bowls and top each with a serving of chicken and a slice of stuffing.

PEPPERED CHICKEN
THIGHS WITH SAGE, HAZELNUTS & NEW POTATOES

Soft green peppercorns are a beautiful addition to this dish. They are gently spiced, more delicate than their black cousins, and sold in jars of brine. Here I've simmered them with whole hazelnuts and new potatoes to make an appealing backdrop to tender poultry thighs.

PREP TIME 15 MINUTES   SERVES 6   COOK TIME 45 MINUTES

12 free-range chicken thighs, with bones and skin

Olive oil, for rubbing onto the thighs

3 red onions, each cut into 8 to 10 wedges

1¾ pounds new potatoes, halved lengthwise

4 garlic cloves, peeled and chopped

1 teaspoon mustard powder

1 tablespoon drained soft green peppercorns in brine, coarsely chopped

2 (14½-ounce) cans diced tomatoes

1⅔ cups hot chicken stock

¾ cup whole hazelnuts

½ bunch (approx. 1½ ounces) of sage leaves

1 Preheat the oven to 350°F.

2 Heat a casserole dish over medium heat. Rub the chicken thighs with olive oil and cook until golden. I'd do this three at a time to avoid overcrowding your pot. Set the golden thighs aside and continue until all have been seen to. Pour away some of the excess fat that may have escaped from the thighs—you just need enough to sauté the onions.

3 Add the onions and sauté for a couple of minutes before adding the potatoes. Cook until the vegetables begin to crisp, 6 to 8 minutes. Add the garlic, mustard powder, and peppercorns and cook for another couple of minutes.

4 Toss in the tomatoes, stock, hazelnuts, and 12 or so sage leaves, coarsely chopped. Return the chicken thighs to the pot, sitting on top of the vegetables, pop the casserole in the oven, and cook, covered, for 30 minutes, followed by 15 minutes with the lid off.

5 When the potatoes are tender and the chicken is cooked through, remove from the oven. Scatter with one or two chopped sage leaves just before serving. Perfect.

PEANUT
CURRIED CHICKEN

We are born knowing that some ingredients belong together: pork and apples, strawberries and cream, eggs and bacon. Others happen upon us later in life and we wish we'd discovered them earlier. May I present sweet potatoes and peanut butter! The potatoes break down during cooking leaving the chicken with a deliciously sweet, thick sauce. Go on, I dare you.

PREP TIME 20 MINUTES   SERVES 6   COOK TIME 40 MINUTES

1 tablespoon vegetable oil

12 skinless, boneless, free-range chicken thighs, kept whole

1 tablespoon butter

2 large red onions, finely sliced

3 garlic cloves, peeled and sliced

1 teaspoon crushed red pepper

3 heaping tablespoons organic crunchy peanut butter

1 tablespoon mild curry paste or 1 teaspoon mild curry powder

1 tablespoon tomato paste

1¾ pounds chunky sweet potatoes, peeled and cut into 1¼-inch cubes

1⅔ cups coconut milk

½ bunch of cilantro, chopped

Sea salt and freshly ground black pepper

1 In a heavy-bottomed saucepan, heat the oil and cook the chicken thighs in batches until each is just beginning to turn golden; this should take a few minutes each side. Set the chicken aside, covered, while you crack on with the base of the recipe.

2 Melt the butter in the saucepan and add the onion, garlic, and crushed red pepper. Sauté over medium heat until soft and steamy but not colored, a couple of minutes. Stir through the peanut butter, curry paste or powder, and tomato paste and heat for another minute. Ensure all the ingredients are nicely incorporated.

3 Add the sweet potatoes, pour over the coconut milk, and give everything a good stir. The coconut milk should reach about halfway up the pan, and don't worry that it doesn't cover the sweet potatoes. Bring to a boil and then reduce the heat to medium. Cover and let the potatoes simmer for 10 minutes.

4 Return the seared chicken thighs to the pot and continue to simmer until the meat is thoroughly cooked through, about 15 minutes. Season as you wish. Just before serving, stir a good clump of chopped cilantro through the pot.

 TIP—IF YOU SUDDENLY DISCOVER YOU ARE OUT OF COCONUT MILK, USE 1½ CUPS LOWFAT MILK AND 3 TABLESPOONS HEAVY CREAM FOR A SLIGHTLY DIFFERENT VERSION OF THIS DISH.

OOZY OVEN-BAKED RICE
WITH TENDER CHICKEN

This recipe is stacked with flavor and has become a Fuggle staple, one of my fall top ten. My recommendation is to use paella rice, but risotto rice is fine, too—both make for a deliciously gloopy accompaniment to the tender chicken legs.

PREP TIME 15 MINUTES	SERVES 4	COOK TIME 45 TO 50 MINUTES

4 free-range chicken legs, skin on

1 tablespoon olive oil

1 large onion, coarsely chopped

7 ounces smoked bacon slices, cut into
 ¾-inch pieces

14 ounces crimini mushrooms, finely sliced

1 cup dry paella rice

3⅓ cups hot chicken stock

3 garlic cloves, peeled and finely chopped

4 tablespoons chopped flat-leaf parsley

Sea salt and freshly ground black pepper

1 Preheat the oven to 325°F.

2 In a large ovenproof, heavy-bottomed saucepan, cook the chicken legs in the oil until crispy and golden. Remove from the pot and set aside.

3 Sauté the onion in the same saucepan until it begins to soften, a minute or so. Add the bacon and pan-fry over high heat, stirring occasionally, until cooked through, then throw in the mushrooms to cook for 2 to 3 minutes. The mushrooms don't need to be crispy; they will cook thoroughly in the oven and it's lovely to have the juices running into the rice.

4 Stir through the rice, stock, garlic, and half of the parsley. Season with salt and black pepper. Nestle the reserved chicken legs in the surface. Pop the lid on and bake in the oven for 45 to 50 minutes, or until the rice is lovely and tender. If you are in the kitchen, give the pot a stir halfway through the cooking time; it's not essential but it does prevent anything from sticking to the bottom of the pot.

5 Remove the pot from the oven and unveil your dinner. Garnish with the rest of the parsley and serve with a green salad, if you wish.

SPANISH CHICKEN
WITH CHORIZO & GARLIC

Years ago I spent a month winding around the railroads of Spain, stopping where the guidebooks spoke of traditional plazas, museums, and fine Spanish cuisine. My memory holds Seville in particular esteem. It must have been to do with the heavily laden orange trees and a supper eaten while watching university students pour out of the library at the most ungodly of hours. I remember eating something similar to this dish and have tried to re-create it, as closely as scribbled notes written by candlelight will allow. *Ole!*

PREP TIME 20 MINUTES   **SERVES 6**   COOK TIME 1 HOUR

1 tablespoon olive oil

6 large free-range chicken thighs, with bones and skin

7 ounces cooking chorizo, cut into ½- to ¾-inch chunks

1 onion, cut into thin wedges

2 medium leeks, chopped into ¾- to 1¼-inch pieces

1 teaspoon Spanish smoked paprika (unsmoked is fine, too)

A pinch of saffron threads

2 whole heads of garlic, cut in half horizontally and left unpeeled

4 sprigs of thyme

½ cup sweet white wine

1 cup hot chicken stock

2 (15-ounce) cans organic lima beans, drained and rinsed

Sea salt and freshly ground black pepper

1 In a large casserole dish, heat the olive oil until smoking hot. Cook the chicken legs on both sides until they are crisp and golden, then transfer to a waiting plate. Keep the heat on high and add the chorizo chunks to the pot. Fry for a minute on each side and remove from the casserole with a slotted spoon so as to leave their oil behind.

2 Add the onion, leeks, and smoked paprika and sauté in the delicious chorizo oil. Reduce the heat, cover, and soften the vegetables, 3 to 4 minutes, but check they don't catch on the bottom of the pot.

3 Add the saffron, garlic halves, thyme, wine, and chicken stock to the pot along with the chicken and chorizo. Season well, cover, and simmer over medium heat for 30 minutes. Let the pot do the work; yours is almost done.

4 Stir in the lima beans and cook for another 10 minutes before serving with a baked potato or two.

LIME ROASTED CHICKEN
WITH POTATOES

Sundays all over the U.K. signal roast chicken lunches and copious platefuls of spuds, but it's easily forgotten that these roasts require an impressive degree of skill—not least managing all the timings and coping with the hungry anticipation. All that juggling has driven me to devise this wonderfully simple, all-in-one method. You may just have enough time to warm your plates!

PREP TIME 15 MINUTES   **SERVES 4**   COOK TIME 1 HOUR 20 MINUTES

1 whole (3¼-pound) free-range chicken

2 whole heads of garlic, cut in half horizontally

1¾ pounds red-skinned potatoes, washed and halved

3 tablespoons mild-tasting olive oil

3 limes, zested and halved

3 plump red chiles, thinly sliced on the diagonal

2 large red onions, each cut into 8 wedges

Sea salt and freshly ground black pepper

1 Preheat the oven to 400°F.

2 Season the cavity of the chicken well and stuff with half a garlic head. Rub the halved potatoes with 1 tablespoon of the olive oil. Use your hands to give them a good coating. Place in a large roasting pan and nestle the chicken in the center. Rub another dash of oil over the chicken and season the skin generously.

3 Place the chicken and potatoes in the center of the oven. After 30 minutes, remove from the oven and reduce the temperature to 350°F.

4 Add all the remaining ingredients to the nest around the chicken and sprinkle over the lime zest. Give the limes a good squeeze over the potatoes (leave the squeezed halves among the potatoes—they look wonderful and will only add flavor) and roast for another 45 minutes, or until the chicken juices run clear.

5 Transfer the chicken to a carving board and let the chicken rest for 10 minutes. Carve and serve with your delicious crusty potatoes and a bowl or two of vegetables.

 TIP—MAKE THE GRAVY IN THE VERY SAME PAN THAT YOU USED TO ROAST THE CHICKEN. SIMPLY REMOVE EVERYTHING, THEN TRANSFER THE PAN TO THE STOVETOP AND PLACE DIRECTLY ON VERY LOW HEAT. SPRINKLE 2 TABLESPOONS ALL-PURPOSE FLOUR OVER THE DELICIOUS CHICKEN JUICES AND STIR UNTIL YOU HAVE A THICK PASTE. VERY GENTLY, ADD 2 CUPS HOT CHICKEN STOCK, MIXING WELL AFTER EACH ADDITION. SEASON AND ADD A SPOT OF MUSTARD SHOULD YOU FEEL THE GRAVY NEEDS IT. THAT'S IT—DONE!

CHICKEN POT PIE

There are few dishes that aren't lifted by a lid of pastry and chicken stew is no exception. The good news is that there's no rubbing of butter into flour, as I've cheated and bought my pie dough from the grocery store (well, at least you're going to make your own sumptuous filling).

PREP TIME 20 MINUTES   SERVES 6   COOK TIME 45 MINUTES

18 ounces puff pastry dough

3 tablespoons butter

3½ cups thinly sliced crimini mushrooms

3 medium leeks, thinly sliced

3 garlic cloves, peeled and finely chopped

1½ pounds skinless, boneless free-range chicken breasts, cut into bite-size chunks

1 tablespoon finely chopped tarragon

1 tablespoon drained soft green peppercorns in brine, coarsely chopped

3 tablespoons all-purpose flour

1¼ cups hot chicken stock

1 free-range egg yolk, beaten

Sea salt and freshly ground black pepper

1 The first step is to roll out the puff pastry dough on a lightly floured work surface until approximately ¼ inch thick. Using a sharp knife, cut around a 2-quart ovenproof pan to create a circle of pastry that will become the lid to your pie. Slide the dough onto a plate and let rest in the fridge while the filling is made.

2 Preheat the oven to 400°F.

3 Melt half of the butter in your chosen pot and cook the mushrooms until they begin to crisp and have lost lots of their moisture. Set aside and add the remaining butter to the pan. Add the leeks and garlic and gently sauté until soft. Take your time doing this; the leeks shouldn't color.

4 Add the chicken pieces to the leeks and cook for 6 to 8 minutes. Your pan will be full to the brim, but that's a

good thing! Return the mushrooms to the pan along with the tarragon and green peppercorns and sprinkle over the flour. Pour over the chicken stock, give everything a good stir to combine, and bring to a simmer. Season to taste.

5 Remove the pan from the heat and place the puff pastry circle over the top, tucking the edges into the pot slightly. Decorate as you wish, traditionally with leaves, or why not go crazy? A pastry chicken could be fun. Use a little beaten egg to stick the decorations on. Make a small hole in the center of the circle so the steam can escape and, working quickly, brush the whole lid with beaten egg.

6 Bake in the oven for 30 minutes, or until the pastry is golden and crisp on top.

CHUBBY CHICKEN LEGS
WITH OLIVES, WHITE WINE & CAPERS

A deceptively simple dish to put together that makes an ideal supper for friends. There is something very comforting about dipping warm bread into juices and sponging up a messy plate—though perhaps you should really only do it in front of those you know very well. My suggestion would be to serve this with a hunk of bread and a glass of chilled white wine.

PREP TIME 10 MINUTES   SERVES 4   COOK TIME 40 MINUTES

3 tablespoons olive oil

5 tablespoons dry white wine

2 large garlic cloves, peeled and very finely sliced

1 cup finely grated Parmesan cheese

4 plump free-range chicken legs, skin on

4 tomatoes, halved

A handful of black olives

2 tablespoons caper berries

Fresh bread, to serve

1 Preheat the oven to 350°F.

2 Put the olive oil, white wine, garlic, and half of the Parmesan into a 2-quart ovenproof dish and stir vigorously to combine. Add the chicken legs and coat well with the sauce. Add the tomatoes, olives, and caper berries to the dish and toss.

3 Turn the chicken so the plump side is facing up and sprinkle with Parmesan to cover, as if with a sheet of snow. Reserve a little of the Parmesan for sprinkling over the finished dish. Cook in the oven for 35 to 40 minutes, or until the chicken meat is pulling away from the bone.

4 Give a final dusting of Parmesan and serve with hunks of bread.

SLOW-COOKED
QUAIL WITH WHEAT BERRIES & BAY

Given that quail sits so beautifully with barley or spelt, it is only a small step farther to partner it with wheat berries, a relatively new ingredient to cross our paths but one that I hope may become more familiar; it is available at whole food markets. When cooked, wheat berries have a subtle, creamy, soft texture with a delicate, nutty taste that complements gamey quail flesh. Feel free to enjoy this one pot heated up after a long, chilly walk. The countryside seasons it wonderfully.

PREP TIME 20 MINUTES SERVES 4 COOK TIME 1 HOUR

3 tablespoons mild-tasting olive oil

4 quail

2 red onions, sliced into thin wedges

2 garlic cloves, peeled and sliced

2 carrots, scrubbed and coarsely chopped

2 celery stalks, finely chopped

1 heaping tablespoon tomato paste

1 cup dry wheat berries (or use pearl barley instead)

2 fresh bay leaves

1 generous sprig of thyme

1¼ cups medium-bodied red wine

2¾ cups fresh chicken stock

A little extra olive oil, for drizzling

Sea salt and freshly ground black pepper

1 In a heavy-bottomed saucepan, heat a dash of the olive oil over medium heat and cook the quail until they have taken on some color. Set them aside, wrapped in foil.

2 Heat the remaining oil in the same pan. Add the onions, garlic, and a small pinch of salt and cook, stirring, for about 5 minutes. Add the carrots, celery, and tomato paste and stir well to combine. Once the vegetables have softened, add the wheat berries (or pearl barley), bay, and thyme.

3 Pour over the wine and half of the chicken stock. Return the quail to the pot and nestle in among everything. Raise the heat slightly to a gentle simmer, then cook, uncovered, for about 30 minutes, stirring every now and then. Add more stock as you need, allowing the wheat berries to absorb the liquid before adding any more.

4 When the wheat berries are nutty and just tender, season well with salt, as they will need it. Stir in a little more olive oil just before serving.

THE FAMOUS
COQ AU VIN

A sociable dish in all regards. Chicken, salty bacon, garlic, nutty mushrooms, and a healthful carafe of wine, left to get to know each other over hours on a hot stove—it's little wonder this combination has made history. Throw in the ingredients and then let the pot perform the introductions. For the best results, marinate the chicken overnight. Serve with some buttered mashed potatoes or a hunk of homemade garlic bread.

PREP TIME 20 MINUTES
(PLUS OVERNIGHT MARINATING)

SERVES 4 TO 6

COOK TIME 1½ HOURS

4 free-range chicken drumsticks and 4 thighs, with bones and skin
2½ cups full-bodied red wine
5 tablespoons brandy
1 bouquet garni (1 sprig of fresh thyme, 1 bay leaf, and 2 fresh sprigs of flat-leaf parsley, tied together with a piece of kitchen twine)
2 tablespoons vegetable oil

7 ounces bacon lardons or bacon slices, chopped
12 shallots, peeled and left whole
3½ cups sliced crimini mushrooms
3 celery stalks, sliced into 1-inch pieces
3 garlic cloves, peeled and sliced
2 tablespoons all-purpose flour
Sea salt and freshly ground black pepper
Fresh flat-leaf parsley, to garnish

1 Place the chicken in a large bowl and pour over the wine and brandy. Nestle in the bouquet garni, cover, and let marinate overnight in the fridge.

2 In a casserole dish, heat 1 tablespoon of the vegetable oil and crisp up the bacon until golden. Lift out of the pot and into a bowl, leaving the fat behind.

3 Next up is the chicken. Remove the chicken from the marinade and pat dry—this will make the skin far easier to brown and will prevent angry oil spitting. If needed, pour a little more oil into the pan and, over medium heat, cook the chicken pieces until the skin is a pale gold. You may have to do this in batches. Set the chicken aside with the

bacon. There will be a deliciously sticky layer clinging to the bottom of the pan, which will provide stacks of flavor, so don't be tempted to clean it.

4 Add the remaining oil to the pot and brown the shallots for a minute before adding the mushrooms, celery, and garlic and sautéing everything for a good 5 minutes. Return the chicken and bacon and sprinkle over the flour. Add the bouquet garni and pour over the marinating liquid. Season with oodles of salt and pepper.

5 Bring to a boil, cover, and simmer gently until the chicken is cooked through, about an hour. Garnish with parsley and serve.

DUCK
WITH RED CURRANTS, PLUMS & PUY LENTILS

Duck boasts an impressively decadent flavor, and I've succumbed to this aura by pairing the breasts with port, plums, and lentils… because nothing else would do.

PREP TIME 15 MINUTES · SERVES 2 · COOK TIME 30 MINUTES

1 tablespoon cornstarch

A good bundle of thyme (about 10 sprigs)

¾ cup port

½ cup hot vegetable stock

2 garlic cloves, peeled and very finely sliced

4 red plums, cut in half and pitted

2 cups cooked Puy lentils

2 duck breast fillets

2 tablespoons red currant jelly

Sea salt and freshly ground black pepper

1 Preheat the oven to 400°F.

2 First things first: pop the cornstarch in a small glass and add approximately 1 tablespoon of water. Stir until you have a smooth paste and set aside.

3 Scatter the thyme sprigs over the bottom of a small roasting pan to form a bed for the duck. Pour over the port, vegetable stock, and cornstarch paste and give a gentle stir. Nestle the garlic slices, plums, and Puy lentils in the pan and cook in the oven for 12 to 15 minutes, until the plums have begun to wilt.

4 Meanwhile, rinse the duck fillets under cold running water and pat them dry with paper towels. Using a sharp knife, make several diagonal slices into the skin, taking care not to slice the meat. Rub the red currant jelly into the skin and season well with salt and pepper. Lay the duck breasts over the plums and lentils, skin-side up, making sure the skin is not submerged in the liquid. Bake in the oven for 15 minutes.

5 While the duck is cooking, preheat the broiler to high. (If your oven and broiler are combined, wait until the 15 minutes are up, then cover the duck in foil so it keeps warm while the broiler heats up.) Place the duck under the broiler for 4 to 5 minutes—this will give you lovely crispy skin.

6 Let the duck sit for a short while, then slice it and serve atop a hill of plums and lentils.

TAKE ONE POT
95

BRAISED DUCK LEGS
WITH JUNIPER & GINGER

We buy chicken legs without too much thought, but duck legs, for no good reason, seem a little more daunting. This intimidation is an urban myth, an old wives' tale, and a conspiracy theory all rolled into one. You'll find below one of the easiest recipes in the whole book—seriously, it can be prepared in moments and then the hard work is left to the oven. I've served the finished dish in a number of ways, so put your own stamp on the recipe and choose if you'd like it hot or cold, in a sandwich, or heaped on a salad.

PREP TIME 10 TO 15 MINUTES   SERVES 4   COOK TIME 2 HOURS

4 large carrots, scrubbed and chopped into approx. ½-inch rounds

5 celery stalks, chopped into ½-inch cubes

2 large onions, coarsely chopped

6 garlic cloves, peeled and finely sliced

2½-inch piece of fresh ginger, peeled and finely chopped

2 teaspoons juniper berries, finely chopped

A dash of vegetable oil

Juice and grated zest of 1 orange

4 duck legs, skin on

2 teaspoons za'atar (optional)

4 to 5 scallions, chopped

Sea salt and freshly ground black pepper

1 Preheat the oven to 350°F.

2 Place all of the chopped vegetables, ginger, and juniper berries in the bottom of a shallow casserole dish and drizzle with a good splash of vegetable oil and the orange juice. (Take a moment to smell the juniper berries and inhale your gin fix without the need for tonic.) Add the orange zest and toss everything thoroughly.

3 Lay the duck legs over the vegetables and season generously with salt and pepper. Sprinkle the za'atar over each leg. Now you've done the hard work, simply pop in

the oven, uncovered, for 1½ to 2 hours depending on the size of your duck legs. The dish is done when the flesh can be pulled away from the bone with the touch of a fork.

4 Take the pot out of the oven and admire your work. Let cool for a few minutes before removing the meat from the legs, using two forks as a means of attack. Shred the flesh and skin and return to your pot.

5 Tumble everything together with the scallions, check for seasoning, and serve as you like.

 TIP—ZA'ATAR IS A WONDERFUL SPICE MIX THAT INCLUDES OREGANO, MARJORAM, TOASTED SESAME SEED, AND SALT. IT'S AVAILABLE AT MIDDLE EASTERN MARKETS AND IS WORTH SEEKING OUT.

CREAMY RABBIT
WITH PLENTY OF HERBS

Yes, rabbits are very sweet and might prompt images of Peter Rabbit, but they do taste extremely good. Make friends with a butcher so he can slip you the youngest, most tender pieces, which will taste a little more spritely than the grandparent. The meat is very lean, so you need to add a little fat when cooking, which helps to give some richness to the recipe.

PREP TIME 20 MINUTES   SERVES 4   COOK TIME 1¼ HOURS

1 to 2 tablespoons olive oil

1½ pounds diced rabbit

1 cup (about 6 ounces) pancetta cubes

1 red onion, coarsely chopped

7 ounces celery root, peeled and cut into ¾-inch chunks

1 (14-ounce) can good-quality plum tomatoes, each tomato squished with the back of a spoon

1 cup hot vegetable stock

2 sprigs of thyme

1 large sprig of rosemary

2 fresh bay leaves

½ cup heavy cream

⅔ cup Kalamata black olives

Flat-leaf parsley, to garnish

1 In a saucepan, heat some of the oil over high heat. Season the rabbit and cook so each piece takes on a golden tinge. Remove the meat and reduce the heat slightly. Add a little more oil to the pan and toss in the pancetta. Pan-fry until just crispy, remove, and set aside with the waiting rabbit.

2 Add the red onion to the pan and gently sauté for 2 to 3 minutes, before adding the celery root chunks and cooking for another 3 to 4 minutes. Return the rabbit and pancetta to the pan, then add the tomatoes, stock, and herbs. Top up with a little water, if needed, so the rabbit is just covered in liquid.

3 Simmer, uncovered, until the rabbit is cooked through, about 45 minutes—older ones may take a little longer. Add the cream to the pot for the final 10 minutes.

4 Just before serving, run the olives through the dish and sprinkle with parsley.

RABBIT POT
WITH MUSTARD & PISTACHIOS

Don't ignore tender rabbit meat when it comes to one pots: the flavor is not dissimilar to that of chicken but with a little more depth, and if you're lucky enough to be given a piece of saddle, the texture will leave you wanting more. The pistachios in this recipe are decadent, but the green nuts taste and look beautiful—include them if you can.

PREP TIME 25 MINUTES   SERVES 6   COOK TIME 1 HOUR

2 rabbits, jointed

3 tablespoons all-purpose flour

3 tablespoons mild-tasting olive oil

1 onion, coarsely chopped

2 garlic cloves, peeled and finely sliced

10½ ounces turnips (about 4), peeled and cut into
    1-inch chunks

4 new-season carrots, scrubbed and cut into
    1-inch chunks

2 sprigs of rosemary

1 heaping tablespoon tomato paste

2 sprigs of tarragon, plus extra to serve

Zest of 1 lemon, peeled into lengths using a
    vegetable peeler

2 tablespoons Dijon mustard

1¼ cups dry hard cider

1¼ cups hot chicken stock

½ cup coarsely chopped pistachios

1 Dust the rabbit pieces with flour, shaking off any excess.

2 In a large casserole dish, heat 2 tablespoons of the oil over high heat. Brown the rabbit pieces on all sides, then remove and set aside.

3 Reduce the heat slightly and add the remaining oil to the pot. Sauté the onion gently until it begins to soften, 5 minutes. Add the garlic and any excess flour you have and cook for another minute, stirring with a wooden spoon. Add the chunks of turnips and carrots and give them a good stir.

4 Return the rabbit to the pot with the rosemary, tarragon, lemon zest, mustard, hard cider, tomato paste, and stock. Slowly bring to a boil, then cover and simmer for 30 minutes. Remove the lid and cook for another 30 minutes.

5 Remove from the heat and sprinkle over the chopped pistachios and some freshly chopped tarragon before serving. The splash of green will look stunning.

VENISON
& CHESTNUT POT

Sophisticated yet easy, this recipe has clambered into my simple dinner repertoire. I like the taste of venison, as it's gamey without being over the top, and wonderfully lean, so good for those who are keeping an eye on their cholesterol levels. My mother makes a lot of stews—it doesn't seem to matter if it's July or December—and so I've learned to enjoy them all year round. Stews give a new lease of life to vegetables that might be lying sad and forgotten in the fridge, and they can also make a small amount of meat stretch to feed a big family. I know why she likes them.

PREP TIME 25 MINUTES   SERVES 4   COOK TIME 2¼ HOURS

2 tablespoons vegetable oil

1½ pounds venison, cut into 1¼-inch dice

2 medium onions, diced, or

    12 whole shallots, peeled

3 garlic cloves, peeled and sliced

3 tablespoons all-purpose flour

2 medium carrots, peeled and cut into ¾-inch chunks

1 small rutabaga, peeled and cut into ¾- to

    1¼-inch cubes

1 or 2 sprigs of thyme

1 or 2 bay leaves

1 cup full-bodied red wine

2 cups good-quality beef stock

1⅔ cups cooked and peeled chestnuts

2 tablespoons cranberry sauce (or red currant jelly

    if it's the wrong time of year)

Chopped flat-leaf parsley, to garnish

Sea salt and freshly ground black pepper

1 In a deep casserole dish, heat the vegetable oil and cook the venison in batches. Each piece should be carefully nurtured: you're aiming for a little caramelizing on each bit of meat, as it will make your stew taste all the richer. Set the browned venison aside on a waiting plate while you crack on with the rest.

2 If necessary, add a little more oil to the pot and sauté the onions and garlic until they are beginning to caramelize, about 5 minutes.

3 Return your delicious venison to the pot and sprinkle over the flour. Give everything a good stir until the flour has all but disappeared. Throw in the carrots, rutabaga, thyme, and bay leaves, pour over the red wine and beef stock, and bring to a simmer. Reduce the heat and allow your pot to gently cook for 1¼ hours.

4 Remove the lid and stir through the chestnuts and cranberry sauce. Season and garnish with some chopped parsley before serving.

PIG POTS

Only those who know me very well will realize this is a special chapter. As a little girl I would request that car journeys be diverted via pig farms so I could pin my face to the window and track the curly pink tails snuffling into their tin houses. My birthday gifts were, on more than one occasion, pictures of the pink princesses or illustrated books teaching me the history of pigs and their importance in British arts. The *pièce de resistance*? Austin, the aged farmer who lived up the road, calling his two enormously spoilt Gloustershire Old Spots Georgina and Caroline, after my sister and me. Never, ever have I felt so proud.

I don't remember discovering that this icon of mine was the source of sausage, lardons, and bacon, but somehow the knowledge only added to my interest.
Within this chapter is a delicious assortment of cuts that create
very yummy dishes to crown any table.

BAKED SAUSAGE
WITH SWEET POTATO & FENNEL

British bangers deserve the iconic status they have been given and I'm only sorry that many of us Brits eat them accompanied by loose "smash" or as blackened crusts from the BBQ. Here is a colorful and hearty fall dish. It's ideal for a midweek supper to show off premium sausage and give it a bit of a makeover.

PREP TIME 15 MINUTES   **SERVES 4**   COOK TIME 45 MINUTES

18 ounces sweet potatoes (approx. 2 large ones), peeled

1 healthy-size fennel bulb

3 garlic cloves, peeled and sliced

1 teaspoon celery seed

1 tablespoon dark brown sugar

3 tablespoons olive oil

8 solid, good-quality sausages

8 smoked Canadian bacon slices

1 tablespoon all-purpose flour

⅓ cup apple juice

4 tablespoons dry white wine

2 tablespoons balsamic vinegar

1 or 2 sprigs of thyme, or fennel fronds if you can find them

Sea salt and freshly ground black pepper

1 Preheat the oven to 400°F. To start, coarsely chop the sweet potato into good 1½-inch chunks and chop the fennel into ½-inch slices across the bulb, then divide into the natural cresents. Place in a large roasting pan with the garlic, celery seed, and brown sugar. Drizzle over the olive oil and give everything a good muddle so all the vegetables are coated. Season well.

2 Wrap each sausage snugly in a slice of bacon so it looks mummified and then nestle in with the vegetables. Roast the whole lot in the oven for 25 minutes.

3 Lightly sprinkle over the flour and jiggle the dish until it's disappeared and has been incorporated among the vegetables. Pour over the apple juice, white wine, and balsamic vinegar, add the herbs, then continue to roast for another 20 minutes until everything is cooked through, the sauce is thickened, and the kitchen is smelling delicious. Serve with a glass of cold hard cider!

MOLASSES BAKED BEANS

There are not many dishes I crave for breakfast, a simple lunch, or indeed a Sunday supper, but this recipe ticks each of these very crucial boxes. It's as versatile as a foldup bicycle on a city commute. I think the key to a wonderfully gloopy dish is laidback, gentle cooking and a generous helping of blackstrap molasses. Make an enormous pot and freeze tubs for those cold, blustery moments when you feel like a hug and there are no hugs to be found.

PREP TIME 20 MINUTES   **SERVES 6**   COOK TIME 7 TO 9 HOURS

2½ cups dry white beans or cannellini beans, rinsed

1 large onion, cut in half

2 fresh bay leaves

½ cup maple syrup

½ cup dark brown sugar

1 tablespoon blackstrap molasses

½ tablespoon crushed red pepper

1 teaspoon salt

1 tablespoon Worcesterhire sauce

1 tablespoon Dijon mustard

7 ounces bacon lardons

1 First, prepare your beans. Put the beans, onion, and bay leaves in a 3½-quart pot and cover with 2¾ quarts cold water. Simmer, uncovered, for about 1 hour, or until the beans are tender. Drain the beans. Discard the onion and bay leaves.

2 To the now-empty pot add the maple syrup, brown sugar, molasses, crushed red pepper, salt, Worcestershire sauce, and Dijon mustard along with 2½ cups water. Bring to a simmer and cook over medium heat until the sauce has come together, a few minutes.

3 Add the beans to the sauce along with the bacon lardons. Let cook on very low heat until the beans melt in your mouth like butter and the sauce has become deliciously syrupy, 6 to 8 hours. Stir as often as you feel like.

 TIP—THESE BEANS FREEZE BEAUTIFULLY, SO DON'T BE SCARED OF MAKING A HUGE BATCH, DIVIDING INTO TUPPERWARE, AND FREEZING FOR LATER IN THE MONTH.

PROSCIUTTO & CHIVE OMELET

PREP TIME 5 MINUTES • COOK TIME 6 MINUTES

Omelets are the ultimate simple supper, especially when the pantry is looking bare. Eggs, a pinch of salt, and one or two other key ingredients are seemingly thrown together like a last-minute outfit, but the results are exquisite (the culinary equivalent of an Oscar ball gown, I suppose).

SERVES 2

4 large free-range eggs, beaten
3 to 4 slices of prosciutto, torn into strips
2 tablespoons finely chopped chives
1½ tablespoons butter
Sea salt and freshly ground black pepper

1 Crack the eggs into a small mixing bowl and lightly beat with a fork. Drop the prosciutto and chives into the bowl and season, season, season.

2 In a medium-size (approx. 8-inch) skillet, heat the butter until it begins to crackle and cover the bottom. Keep the heat high and pour in the egg mixture. With a spatula at the ready, draw the outside edges (which will cook more quickly) toward the gooey center. Allow any liquid mixture to move into the gaps.

3 Continue with this action for about 2 minutes; don't forget that the omelet will continue to cook once the pan is removed from the heat.

4 Fold the omelet in half and divide between two plates, as neatly as you wish, then serve with a spot of salad.

PEA, PROSCIUTTO & MINT FRITTATA

PREP TIME 10 MINUTES • COOK TIME 15 MINUTES

The glorious frittata is perfect for summer picnics.

MAKES 6 BIG TRIANGLES

2 tablespoons olive oil
1 medium onion, coarsely chopped
2 garlic cloves, peeled and finely chopped
½ teaspoon cayenne pepper
9 medium free-range eggs
1 cup frozen peas
Heaping ¾ cup finely grated Parmesan cheese
3 tablespoons coarsely chopped mint
6 slices of prosciutto, torn into strips
Sea salt and freshly ground black pepper

1 In a 9-inch nonstick skillet, heat half of the oil, add the onion, and sauté until translucent, then add the garlic and cayenne and cook for 1 minute. Remove from the pan and cool slightly.

2 Crack the eggs into a large bowl and gently mix. Stir through the onion, frozen peas, three-quarters of the Parmesan, and the mint. This is your opportunity to season radically, so crack that pepper. Stir well to combine. Preheat the broiler to high.

3 Place the pan back on low heat and add the remaining olive oil. Heat for about 30 seconds. Pour the egg mixture into the pan in a gorgeous heap and lie the prosciutto strips on the surface. Gently cook until the underside is firm and the frittata is cooked ½ to ¾ inch from the edge but the center is still a little wobbly, about 10 minutes. Sprinkle over the remaining Parmesan.

4 Transfer the pan to the broiler and cook until the top is golden and puffed like a peacock. Don't overcook, as the frittata will continue to cook in the residual heat. Remove and let cool for a few minutes before serving in wedges.

MANCHEGO, PANCETTA
& LEEK RISOTTO

Risotto is a blank canvas that is dressed according to your mood—this punchy combination of manchego and pancetta oozes sophistication and catapults a humble risotto into a meal worthy of royalty, or even just a very good friend.

PREP TIME 10 MINUTES   **SERVES 2**   COOK TIME 35 MINUTES

2 tablespoons olive oil

2 small leeks, chopped into ¼-inch rounds

Heaping ½ cup diced smoked pancetta

A pat of butter

1 cup dry Arborio or Carnaroli risotto rice

3½ cups hot chicken stock

2 tablespoons red pesto

½ cup shredded Manchego cheese

Sea salt and freshly ground black pepper

1 In a deep sauté pan, heat 1 tablespoon of the olive oil over high heat. Add the leeks and pancetta to the pan and cook until the leeks are looking tender and the pancetta is cooked through, 4 to 5 minutes. Remove from the pan and set aside.

2 Add the remaining olive oil and the pat of butter to the pan and reduce the heat to low. Add the risotto rice and stir so the grains are coated in the oily butter. Gradually add all but ⅓ cup of the hot stock, one ladleful at a time, stirring each until it's absorbed before you think of adding the next; this will take about 25 minutes, so go slowly. Season to taste.

3 When the risotto is al dente and the whole thing is looking sloppy, stir through the pesto and return the leeks and bacon to the pan (reserving a few pieces for garnish). Warm the risotto through and add the remaining ⅓ cup hot chicken stock if you think it's needed. Remove from the heat, stir through the Manchego, and serve with the reserved leeks and pancetta and a good twist of black pepper on the top.

 TIP—IF YOU MAKE YOUR RISOTTO IN ADVANCE, STOP COOKING THE RICE A FEW MINUTES BEFORE IT'S DONE AND LET COOL. TO SERVE, HEAT A PAN WITH A FEW SPOONFULS OF STOCK IN THE BOTTOM AND, WHEN BUBBLING, SPOON IN THE RISOTTO. CONTINUE TO ADD HOT STOCK UNTIL THE RICE IS COOKED AND THE CONSISTENCY IS THAT OF THICK PORRIDGE.

SPINACH, SALAMI & FETA QUESADILLAS

PREP TIME 5 MINUTES • COOK TIME 8 MINUTES

A quesadilla is the Mexican equivalent of that great favorite the toasted cheese sandwich—and I would say it definitely has the edge for three reasons. First, in order to make it you don't need a machine that gathers dust for the majority of the year. Second, the quesadilla has an endearing communal feel about it, one large round being sliced into equal triangles. Third, generally the fillings are more varied. It's my food of choice for watching some sport or, more likely, a good old period drama on television.

SERVES 4

2 large flour tortillas
1⅔ cups baby spinach
5 or 6 slices of salami, each torn roughly into 3
⅓ cup crumbled feta cheese
⅓ cup finely grated sharp cheddar cheese
Sea salt and freshly ground black pepper

1 Here it is—just the one step, but make sure all the ingredients are ready, as you don't have long once the pan is hot! Heat up a skillet large enough to hold a tortilla. Once it's hot, place the tortilla in the bottom of the pan (no oil needed) and sprinkle the ingredients on the top with a good grinding of black pepper. Sandwich with the other tortilla and cook until the bottom one starts to turn golden, about 4 to 5 minutes. Being careful, flip it over (I may use a large cutting board placed over the skillet to help me do this). Cook the other side for a couple of minutes. Done in less than 10 minutes. Now turn on the TV and cut the quesadilla into quarters to serve.

PUMPKIN PACKETS WITH BACON & SAGE

PREP TIME 10 MINUTES • COOK TIME 1 TO 1¼ HOURS

For a few weeks every year shelves are inundated with pumpkins awaiting their callous fate of becoming contorted expressions. If you do resist the urge to grab a scalpel and opt to cook your pumpkin instead, here is a super-simple suggestion. The baked crescents could be eaten for lunch just so or served with some grilled or broiled sausage for an easy dinner.

SERVES 6

2¼ pounds pumpkin, seeded and cut into 4 to 5 wedges (leave the skin on)
12 to 14 bacon slices
12 sage leaves
2 tablespoons extra virgin olive oil
Sea salt and freshly ground black pepper
A drizzle of maple syrup and corn salad, to serve

1 Preheat the oven to 325°F.

2 Wrap each pumpkin wedge in 3 or 4 slices of bacon and weave the sage leaves among the bacon.

3 Lie the wrapped edges on a lightly oiled baking sheet and then drizzle with the olive oil. Season and bake in the oven for 1 to 1¼ hours, until the pumpkin is tender. Serve drizzled with maple syrup aboard a pile of corn salad.

HAM, MUSTARD
& PARSLEY TARTIFLETTE

There is a logical association linking tartiflette to cold French mountains—not many recipes can deliver such a concentration of calories that keeps skiers flying down the slopes until dusk. I would argue that a harsh frost anywhere in the world renders us all in need of a good tartiflette. This one has salty ham and Camembert hidden within the potato layers and is ideal for stomachs that require energy loading. A healthful green salad is all that is needed to accompany it.

PREP TIME 20 MINUTES   SERVES 6   COOK TIME 2 HOUR

A little oil, for greasing

2¼ pounds waxy potatoes, peeled

1 large onion, peeled

Approx. 3 thick slices of cooked ham (7 ounces), torn

1 whole (9-ounce) Camembert cheese, torn into ¾-inch chunks

3 tablespoons coarsely chopped flat-leaf parsley, plus 1 tablespoon to serve

1 tablespoon Dijon mustard

¾ cup plus 1 tablespoon hot vegetable stock

1¼ cups heavy cream

Sea salt and freshly ground black pepper

1 Preheat the oven to 350°F. Brush the inside of a generous 2-quart ovenproof dish with olive oil.

2 Your first job is to do the slicing. Start with the potatoes, which need to be about ¼ inch thick; you will need a steady hand and a sharp knife or a food processor. Next are the onions, again ¼ inch thick.

3 Now it's as easy as a dot-to-dot. Start by placing about a fifth of the potato slices on the bottom of the ovenproof dish. Season and then layer with about a quarter of the ham, onion rings, torn Camembert, and parsley. Top with another fifth of potato slices and, using your hands, apply a bit of pressure to compress the layer. Continue with the other layers until all the ingredients have been used up. By my estimation there will be four layers, and then a final layer of potato slices.

4 Dot the top with mustard and gently pour over the hot stock and then the cream. Season again. Cover with greased foil (this is important, or the foil will stick to the potatoes) and bake in the oven for 1 hour. Remove the foil and sprinkle over the remaining parsley. Bake, uncovered, for 1 more hour.

5 Remove the dish from the oven and let sit in a warm place for 20 to 30 minutes before serving. It will still be perfectly hot but everything will have "come to."

HAM HOCK
LIMA BEAN & PARSLEY BROTH

You could be forgiven for feeling some confusion at the butcher's counter as pork shanks, ham hocks, and pig knuckles, are all the same cut; in other words, you can use any of them. The masses haven't quite cottoned on to this cut, so it's still wonderfully cheap to buy and two or three hocks can feed an army.

PREP TIME 20 MINUTES   **SERVES 6 TO 8**   COOK TIME 4 HOURS

2 ham hocks (each weighing 2¼ to 3¼ pounds)
1 large onion, coarsely chopped
3 plump garlic cloves, peeled and sliced
3 celery stalks, cut into 1¼-inch chunks

3 large carrots, peeled and cut into 1¼-inch chunks
1 bunch of flat-leaf parsley, stems chopped and
   leaves kept for garnish
2 (15-ounce) cans lima beans, drained

1 Put the ham hocks into a 5¼-quart saucepan and cover with cold water. Bring to a boil and let bubble for 10 minutes. Drain away the scummy water and refill the pot with 3¼ quarts cold water.

2 Bring the fresh water to a boil and gently simmer, uncovered, skimming the residue occasionally, until the ham is cooked and the meat is falling off the bone, 2½ hours. Add the onion, garlic, celery, carrots, and parsley stems to the pot and stir through the beautiful ham stock. Remove the lid and cook for 1 more hour.

3 Remove the ham hocks from the pot using an enormous spoon or tongs and, once they are cool enough to handle, pick out the big chunks of meat and discard the fat and

bones; the meat should fall easily off the bone. Don't be alarmed by the surprising amount of fat on these knuckles. Using your fingers, tear the ham into bite-size shreds.

4 Return the shredded ham to the pot and add the lima beans. Simmer to allow the beans to break down slightly, 5 to 10 minutes, then remove from the heat. The consistency should be gloopy and that of a thick broth, so continue to boil if the stock needs to reduce more.

5 Just before serving, garnish with the parsley leaves and season as required. My vote would be to serve this in warmed shallow bowls with some fluffy warm bread.

 TIP—DON'T BE SURPRISED IF YOU RETURN TO ANY LEFTOVERS THE FOLLOWING DAY AND FIND THE GELATIN HAS SET THE BROTH SOLID. SIMPLY REHEAT OVER LOW HEAT AND YOU'RE BACK IN BUSINESS FOR SECONDS.

PORK & PISTACHIO MEATLOAF

PREP TIME 20 MINUTES • COOK TIME 35 MINUTES

A cluster of recipes have been tarnished by associations with wartime, and sadly meatloaf is one of them. But this dish is due for a makeover and needs to be firmly pinned back on the culinary map. Let's look at the positives: it can be eaten hot or cold, summer or winter, it's super-quick to do, inexpensive to make, and wonderfully nutritious to eat. I've stuffed flavor into this recipe and it's begging to be given a shot.

MAKES 10 SLICES

2¼ cups fresh, white bread crumbs

1⅓ cups coarsely chopped pistachios

2¼ pounds ground pork

⅓ cup chopped pickled gherkins

1 tablespoon English mustard

3 garlic cloves, peeled and crushed

2 medium free-range eggs, beaten

Sea salt and freshly ground black pepper

Fresh thyme, to serve

1 Preheat the oven to 350°F. Line the bottom of a 2-pound nonstick loaf pan with wax paper.

2 Combine all of the ingredients in one enormous bowl. Get your hands involved to really squish everything together. Season, season, season.

3 Pack down the mixture into the loaf pan as best you can and bake in the oven for 35 minutes, until the loaf is firm to the touch. Allow it to "come to" for about 10 minutes before turning it out. Let cool, then slice and serve with the pickled cucumber (see right) and a sprig of fresh thyme.

PICKLED CUCUMBER

PREP TIME 10 MINUTES (PLUS 1 HOUR COOLING)
• COOK TIME 10 MINUTES

Try this lip-smacking pickle with your meatloaf.

MAKES 1 (9-OUNCE) JAR

4 tablespoons white wine vinegar

Juice of 1 lime

1 tablespoon black mustard seed

3 tablespoons superfine sugar

½ tablespoon salt

½ medium cucumber, cut into ¼-inch slices on the angle

3½ ounces radishes, trimmed and large ones cut in half

A small clump of fennel fronds or 1 tablespoon chopped dill weed

1 Simply place the vinegar, lime juice, mustard seed, salt, and sugar in a small saucepan. Bring to a simmer and stir until the sugar dissolves, a minute or so. Let cool.

2 Squeeze the cucumber, radishes, and fennel fronds (or dill weed) into your waiting, sterilized canning jar and pour over the pickling liquid. Seal tightly and wait for at least 4 hours before tucking in.

ROSE HARISSA PORK

WITH QUINOA & DATES

Eeeshhh… there's a fine line between cooking pork tenderloin too much (when the meat will be as dry as a bone) or too little, when it'll be too pink—and too pink pork isn't good for anybody. I've cooked this recipe, in which the pork is covered and nestled among quinoa, stock, and juicy dates, so there should be no danger of tough meat. It's a beautiful recipe, a slightly different take on a tagine. My husband said it was "damn good," which I think is a thumbs up.

PREP TIME 10 MINUTES   SERVES 2 TO 3   COOK TIME 35 MINUTES

1 tablespoon olive oil

11 to 14 ounces pork tenderloin

1 medium onion, coarsely chopped

1½ tablespoons rose harissa paste

Scant ⅔ cup dry quinoa

½ cup pitted dried dates, coarsely chopped

3 large, ripe tomatoes, coarsely chopped

1⅔ cups hot chicken stock

4 tablespoons coarsely chopped flat-leaf parsley

Sea salt and freshly ground black pepper

1 Preheat the oven to 350°F.

2 In a shallow, ovenproof pot, heat the oil over high heat. Season your meat and, using tongs, sear the pork on all sides until beautifully golden. Remove from the pot and set aside to rest.

3 Add a drop more oil to the pot if needed and sauté the onion until translucent, a few minutes, then stir through the harissa. Add the quinoa, dates, tomatoes, and just 1¼ cups of the hot stock. Give everything a good stir, season well, and simmer for 10 minutes. Stir through the remaining stock and half of the parsley once the 10 minutes are up.

4 Place the pork tenderloin on top of your quinoa mixture and place the pot in the oven for 20 minutes, covered, until the quinoa is plump and the pork is cooked through. Remove from the oven and let the dish sit so the pork can rest and "come to," 5 to 7 minutes

5 Sprinkle generously with the rest of the parsley, and serve the pork sliced on a bed of quinoa.

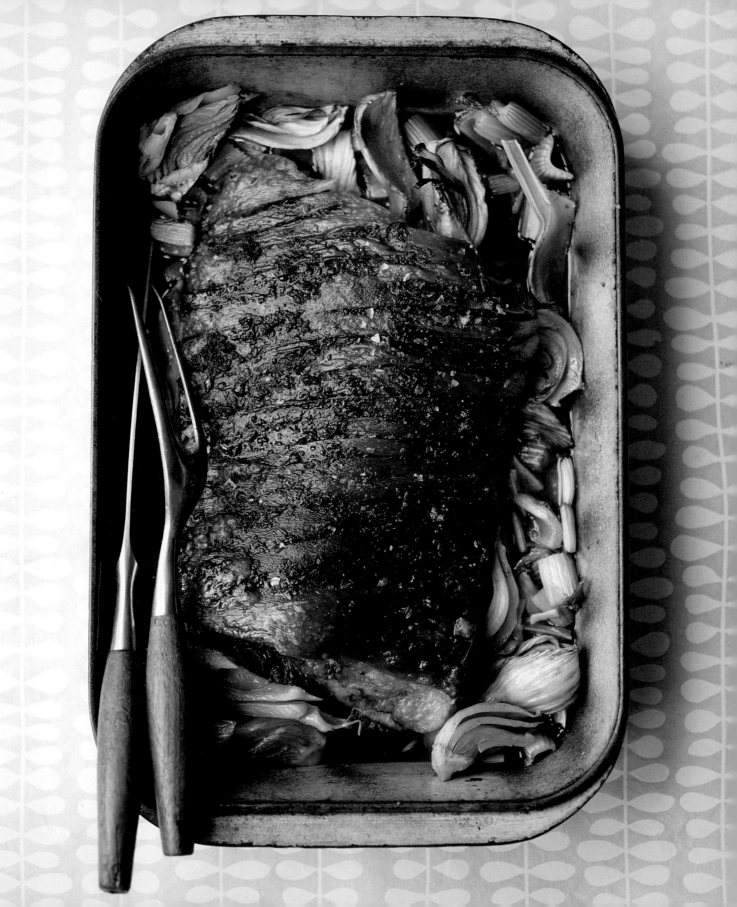

MELTING POT BELLY
WITH FENNEL & ROSEMARY

When cooked correctly, pork belly has a blistered skin that cracks, brittle like an icy puddle, fat that renders to a glorious slush, and meat that pulls apart with the slightest nudge. This dish isn't difficult, so should help you to achieve just that—I have a wonderful friend who unashamedly stole this recipe and cooked it four times in as many dinner parties, achieving perfection each and every time.

PREP TIME 10 MINUTES — SERVES 4 TO 6 — COOK TIME 3½ HOURS

3¼ pounds boneless pork belly

1 tablespoon sea salt

1 tablespoon finely chopped rosemary

1 tablespoon olive oil

1 red onion, cut into quarters

10 to 12 garlic cloves, peeled and cut in half

2 fennel bulbs, cut into 1¼-inch wedges

3 celery stalks, cut into large chunks

2 cups hot chicken stock

Freshly ground black pepper

Crème fraîche, to serve

1 Preheat the oven to 425°F. Using a sharp knife, score the skin of your pork belly in diagonal lines approximately 1 inch apart, taking care only to score the fat and not cut into the meat. Rub the sea salt and rosemary deep into the fat and season with black pepper. Drizzle with olive oil.

2 Place the belly in a roasting dish that's big enough for the meat to lie flat and roast in the oven for about 30 minutes. You will see the skin start to become crispy crackling. After 30 minutes, turn the heat down to 350°F and roast for 1 hour more.

3 Remove the meat from the oven and carefully place it on a board. Reduce the oven temperature to 325°F. Tip all the vegetables into the roasting dish and smother with the fat. Pour the stock into the roasting dish. Return the belly back to the top of the vegetables and roast in the oven for another 1½ to 2 hours. The pork is ready to serve when it almost falls away to the touch.

4 Once it's wonderfully tender, remove the pork from the dish and cut into chunks with a sharp knife. Serve with the braised vegetables and a large spoonful of crème fraîche.

CARAMELIZED PORK

CHORIZO & BLOOD SAUSAGE STEW (FABADA ASTURIANA)

My first taste of *fabada asturiana* was sitting in a rustic Spanish restaurant. Formica tables and red plastic bread baskets colored the room in which a round woman ladled the only menu choice into shallow bowls, spilling precious stock as she went. I asked for the recipe and here it is, with one or two tweaks that may have been lost in translation.

PREP TIME 30 MINUTES
(PLUS OVERNIGHT SOAKING)   SERVES 8   COOK TIME 3 HOURS

2½ cups dry white beans

14 ounces pork shoulder blade roast, cut into
    1¼- to 1½-inch chunks

7 ounces cooking chorizo

1 (5½-ounce) blood sausage

6 to 8 smoked bacon slices

1 onion, finely sliced

2 carrots, peeled and chopped

A few saffron threads

Sprigs of flat-leaf parsley, to garnish

1 Now, you'll have to think ahead a bit for this one and get going the evening before your dish is needed. Soak the white beans overnight in a bowl of cold water and soak the pork in another.

2 When you are ready to begin, drain the beans and put into a 4¼- to 5¼-quart pot. Cover with fresh cold water. Bring to a boil and simmer over gentle heat for about an hour, skimming off any residue on the surface.

3 Add the drained pork, chorizo, blood sausage, bacon, onion, carrots, and saffron. Add a bit more cold water, making sure all the ingredients are just submerged, and bring back to a simmer. Cook until the meat and beans are perfectly tender, about 2 hours. Stir occasionally to make sure the bottom isn't catching.

4 Remove the pot from the heat and fish out the blood sausage, chorizo, and bacon. Once they have cooled slightly, slice up into small chunks and set aside. (In Spain, this mixture is traditionally known as the *compango*.)

5 Ladle some beans and liquid into your serving bowls and top with a selection of the *compango*. Sprinkle with oodles of parsley and serve.

PIG CHEEKS
WITH CARROTS & HARD CIDER

My very patient husband has eaten with me throughout writing this book and if he were to pick his favorite dish this would win gold. Pig cheeks (jowls), which are exquisite pillows of tender pork about the size of a halved plum, should be cooked when you aren't in a rush and have time to enjoy the preparation. It is obvious that they sit sublimely well alongside a good splash of hard cider and some scented thyme.

PREP TIME 25 MINUTES   SERVES 4   COOK TIME 2¾ HOURS

2 tablespoons vegetable oil

2¼ pounds pig cheeks

Scant 1 cup pancetta lardons

2 onions, finely sliced

1 teaspoon ground ginger

3 carrots, peeled and cut into bite-size chunks

½ large celery root, peeled and chopped into
 bite-size chunks

2 garlic cloves, peeled and sliced

2 tablespoons all-purpose flour

A bundle of thyme, tied together with kitchen twine

2 cups hard cider

1¼ cups vegetable stock

3 tablespoons heavy cream

1 tablespoon whole grain mustard

Sea salt and freshly ground black pepper

Pea shoots (dau miu) or flat-leaf parsley, chopped,
 to garnish

1 In a large, heavy-bottomed pan, heat the oil over high heat, and cook the pig cheeks, 4 or 5 at a time, until browned on both sides. Remove from the pan and set aside. Pan-fry the pancetta until crispy and set aside with the cheeks.

2 Lower the heat and gently sauté the onions with the ground ginger until soft; you may need to add a touch more oil. Add the carrots, celery root, and garlic and cook until they begin to soften, a few minutes. Return the pig cheeks and lardons to the pot and sprinkle over the flour. Stir to coat until you can no longer see the flour.

3 Throw in the bundle of thyme, the hard cider, and vegetable stock. Season and bring to a simmer, then reduce the heat, cover, and cook for 2½ hours. Remove the lid for the last 30 minutes.

4 With a large slotted spoon, remove all "the bits" so you can finish off the sauce. Pour in the cream and mustard. Bring the liquid to a boil and let bubble until the sauce has thickened, about 10 minutes. Return all the meat to the pot and serve garnished with a pile of pea shoots or freshly chopped parsley.

FOUR HOOVES: BEEF & LAMB

The old proverb, "God sends meat and the devil sends cooks," seems particularly apt when we're faced with a filet mignon or lamb loin roast. Pressure is on from the moment the quite large wad of cash is handed over and really it's only the chef to be blamed if something goes wrong. Stewing meat, on the other hand, marbled with fat and stacked with flavor, is certainly more forgiving and relies a bit more on the ingredients it mingles with. Initially there is slightly more work, but once you've done the chopping, making a slow-cooked pot requires less effort than going as yourself to a fancy dress party.

Hidden among these recipes are cuts that you will almost certainly be familiar with, but I hope I can also encourage you to try the odd beef or lamb shank. They create wonderful centerpieces that will make any recipient love you that much more.

BURGUNDY BEEF
WITH STILTON DUMPLINGS

Of course you can make this recipe with another red wine, perhaps Merlot or Malbec, but I believe the richer the wine, the more delicious the end result. Paired with the Silton dumplings and a dash of brandy, this is a gentleman's club embodied in an honored stew. All that's needed is a post-dinner cigar and a smoking jacket.

PREP TIME 30 MINUTES   **SERVES 6**   COOK TIME 2½ HOURS

2 tablespoons olive oil

2¼ pounds boneless beef shank, trimmed of fat
    and cut into 1¼-inch cubes

2 onions, coarsely chopped

2 tablespoons all-purpose flour, seasoned

4 garlic cloves, peeled and cut in half

4 carrots, scrubbed and cut into 1¼-inch lengths

4 small parsnips, scrubbed, chopped lengthwise,
    and then into chunks

3 to 4 sprigs of thyme

2 cups Burgundy

2 tablespoons brandy

2 cups beef stock

FOR THE DUMPLINGS

1 cup self-rising flour

3½ tablespoons butter, softened

⅓ cup crumbled Stilton or other blue cheese

1 tablespoon coarsely chopped flat-leaf parsley

3 to 4 tablespoons cold water

1 In a deep casserole dish, heat the oil over high heat. Sear the beef in batches until each piece has begun to caramelize, then set aside. Add the onions to the pot, reduce the heat slightly, and sauté until soft. Return the meat to the pot, sprinkle with the flour, and stir to combine.

2 Add the garlic, carrots, parsnips, thyme, wine, brandy, and beef stock to the pot (i.e everything else). Bring to simmering point, reduce the heat, then cover and simmer for 2½ hours. Every so often give your stew a good stir to stop it sticking to the bottom of the pan. And don't be afraid to add a little water if you think it's looking dry, as every stove cooks at a slightly different temperature.

3 Meanwhile, make the dumplings. Rub the butter into the flour and mix with the cheese and parsley. Add enough cold water to bring the mixture together to a soft dough and divide into 5 or 6 dumplings.

4 Fifteen minutes before the end of the stew's cooking time, drop the dumplings onto its surface and continue to cook, covered, until the clouds puff and you have edible blotting paper, a final 15 minutes. Serve.

SOY CHILE BEEF

This Asian-inspired casserole uses lean steak which, though a little more expensive, makes for a super-speedy supper option. If you suddenly have six hungry mouths to feed, don't be afraid to make it stretch with a bit more sweet potato. Serve with steamed rice.

PREP TIME 15 MINUTES | SERVES 4 | COOK TIME 25 MINUTES

2 tablespoons vegetable oil

2 onions, coarsely chopped

3 garlic cloves, peeled and finely chopped

2 tablespoons all-purpose flour

1 teaspoon five-spice powder

2 to 3 star anise

3 red bell peppers, seeded and cut into chunky strips

1 large or 2 medium sweet potatoes (about 18 ounces cubed weight), peeled and cut into 1¼-inch chunks

2 red chiles, seeded and finely chopped, or
   2 teaspoons crushed red pepper

2 tablespoons dark brown sugar

3 tablespoons dark soy sauce

2½ cups hot beef stock

1 pound boneless top sirloin steak, cut into
   thin, bite-size strips (best sliced across the grain)

A small handful of cilantro sprigs, to garnish

Freshly ground black pepper

1 In a heavy-bottomed casserole dish, heat the vegetable oil over high heat. Add the onion, reduce the heat to medium, and soften for approximately 5 minutes, adding in the garlic for the last minute.

2 Stir through the flour, then throw in the five-spice, star anise, bell peppers, sweet potatoes, and chiles (or crushed red pepper). Sprinkle with the brown sugar, season with black pepper, and heat through for a minute or so.

3 Add the soy sauce and beef stock and bring to a boil. Reduce the heat, cover, and simmer until the sweet potatoes are tender, about 15 minutes. Add the beef strips to the pot for the final 5 minutes of this time. Cover and simmer until they just cook in the broth and are beautifully tender.

4 Top each serving with a pert sprig of cilantro.

 TIP—TRY USING TENDER CHICKEN INSTEAD OF THE BEEF AND REMOVING THE CHILES TO MAKE THIS BROTH SUITABLE FOR LITTLE PEOPLE.

BEEF, PRUNE
& ROSEMARY CASSEROLE

Like French cheese and wildflower meadows, some stews (most, in fact) mature with age. After a day or two in the fridge, richer and sweeter notes come dancing through. With this recipe in particular, the delicate sugars of the prunes take hold and the steak becomes ever more tender, so think ahead, fellow cooks, and start preparing.

PREP TIME 20 MINUTES   **SERVES 6**   COOK TIME 2½ HOURS

3 tablespoons vegetable oil

9 ounces pancetta, cut into ½-inch cubes

1¾ pounds chuck steak or stewing beef, diced

14 ounces shallots, peeled but kept whole

4¼ cups thickly sliced crimini mushrooms

4 garlic cloves, peeled and each cut into 3

1⅓ cups pitted prunes, halved

2 tablespoons all-purpose flour

5 tablespoons sherry vinegar

3⅓ cups hot beef stock

4 to 5 sprigs of rosemary, plus extra for sprinkling

1½ pounds Maris Piper potatoes, sliced into thin (⅛-inch) rounds

Sea salt and freshly ground black pepper

1 Preheat the oven to 375°F.

2 In a casserole dish, heat 1 tablespoon of the oil. Start with the pancetta and pan-fry until it's crispy and smells like Sunday mornings. Set aside and continue with the beef. Cook this in two or three batches so the pan doesn't overcrowd, and keep the heat up so the meat browns, adding more oil when needed. This will take a few minutes, but don't be tempted to miss out this step and "make do" with only gray meat. You'll taste the color. Remove the beef from the casserole and set aside with the pancetta.

3 Next up are the shallots. Sauté until the edges begin to brown. Remove and add to the waiting meat. Finally, cook the mushrooms over high heat until crispy, adding in the garlic for the last minute or so.

4 Return the beef, pancetta, and shallots to the pan and add the prunes. Stir through the flour and season well. Pour over the sherry vinegar and let it bubble off before adding the stock and rosemary sprigs. Cook, covered, in the oven for 1 hour.

5 Arrange your potato slices on the surface of the stew like the apples on a French apple tart. Season again, sprinkle with chopped rosemary, and return to the oven for 30 minutes. Remove the lid and cook until the potatoes are tender, 30 minutes. Serve piping hot.

 TIP—IF YOU ARE IN A HURRY, BLANCH YOUR SLICED POTATOES AND ADD THEM TO THE TOP OF THE CASSEROLE—THEY SHOULD ONLY TAKE 20 MINUTES TO COOK THROUGH.

POT-ROAST BRISKET
WITH PORCINI & BARLEY

Here is a really impressive one pot with oodles of flavor and a variety of ingredients that may push you to step out of your comfort zone. The barley loves being cooked for so long and results in hundreds of plump cushions supporting the tender beef.

PREP TIME 20 MINUTES   SERVES 6   COOK TIME 3½ HOURS

1 cup dried porcini mushrooms

2 to 3 tablespoons olive oil

3¼- to 4-pound rolled beef brisket

2 medium onions, coarsely chopped

3 garlic cloves, peeled and sliced

½ teaspoon crushed red pepper

1 cup dry pearl barley

2 tablespoons (¼ stick) butter

3 sprigs of rosemary

5 cups hot beef stock

Sea salt and freshly ground black pepper

1 Soak the porcini in 2 cups boiling water for 30 minutes. Remove the mushrooms, reserving the precious liquid, and squeeze dry in your hands. Finely chop and set aside.

2 Preheat the oven to 325°F.

3 Place a deep, 5¼-quart casserole dish over high heat. Add the olive oil and, using tongs to steady the meat, brown the beef all over. Remove and set aside to a waiting plate. Reduce the heat slightly and add the chopped onions, garlic, and crushed red pepper. Cook until the onion has softened and you can smell the garlic, 4 to 5 minutes. Season with salt and freshly ground black pepper.

4 Stir through the pearl barley and butter. Add the chopped porcini to the pot with their cooking liquid and throw in the rosemary. Nestle the browned beef in the center of the pot and pour the hot beef stock around, taking care not to pour on top of the meat. Stir gently to make sure all the ingredients are perfectly combined and cover with a tight-fitting lid. Cook in the oven for 3 hours, stirring once or twice to ensure nothing is catching on the bottom of the pot.

5 When you finally remove the pot from the oven and unveil the roast, stir through a bit of boiling water to loosen the barley, if you think it's necessary. I would suggest removing the beef from the pot in order to slice it, before plating up with a good spoonful of the barley.

BEEF, LENTIL
& GREEN OLIVE STEW

I've given this stew a bit of personality. The base is one you'll be familiar with, but note the addition of lentils, ground cloves, and olives. Lentils will enrich the sauce, while the olives do the seasoning for you with an Italian salty bite to enhance a thoroughly British classic. Make it in advance if you know you are in for a busy weekend. This dish doesn't mind being kept waiting.

PREP TIME 40 MINUTES   **PLENTY FOR 8**   COOK TIME 2½ HOURS

2 tablespoons olive oil

3¼ pounds chuck steak or stewing beef, trimmed of fat
  and cut into 1¼- to 1½-inch pieces

14 ounces shallots

3 tablespoons seasoned all-purpose flour

½ teaspoon cayenne pepper

¼ teaspoon ground cloves

1¼ cups medium-bodied red wine

3 celery stalks, chopped into 1¼-inch pieces

3 fresh bay leaves

2 garlic cloves, peeled but kept whole

2 cups hot beef stock

1¾ pounds tomatoes, chopped

1 cup dry Puy lentils

Scant 1 cup fat green olives

Sea salt

Freshly chopped flat-leaf parsley, to garnish

Sour cream, to serve

1 In a large casserole dish, heat the oil and cook the beef in batches until golden brown all over, adding an extra dash of oil with every new batch if you feel it needs it. Remove the meat from the pot and set aside.

2 Meanwhile, put the shallots in a large bowl. Cover with boiling water and let soak for a few minutes, then drain and cool down by placing in cold water. Peel, trim the bases, and cut any large shallots in half. Add to the casserole and cook until just beginning to caramelize, about 3 to 4 minutes.

3 Return the browned beef to the pan and sprinkle over the flour, cayenne pepper, and ground cloves. Stir until the flour and spices are all incorporated. Add the red wine,

bring to a boil, and let bubble until the alcohol has evaporated, a minute or so. Reduce the heat to low and add the celery, bay leaves, garlic, beef stock, chopped tomatoes, and lentils to the pot. Give your stew a little pinch of salt—you won't need any pepper because the cayenne ticks that box.

4 Cover with a tight-fitting lid and simmer, on low heat, for 1½ hours, stirring occasionally to make sure the bottom of the stew isn't catching. Remove the lid and add the olives 30 minutes before the end of cooking.

5 Garnish with chopped parsley and serve with a large spoonful of sour cream.

WARMING BEEF SHANK
WITH CRUNCHY MUSTARD CROUTONS

Beef shank has fabulous strips of collagen keeping all the muscles together, which melt to form a sticky stew, so don't be alarmed when you first glance at the meat (some would say fat equals flavor!). You could make the stew in advance and just add the croutons on the night to make this an easy yet thoroughly entertaining recipe. Serve with a good pile of mashed potatoes for a seriously hearty supper.

PREP TIME 30 MINUTES | SERVES 6 | COOK TIME 3½ HOURS

3¼-pound piece of beef shank, cut into
    1½- to 2-inch pieces
4 tablespoons vegetable oil
3 large onions, thickly sliced
4 to 5 garlic cloves, peeled and sliced
2 tablespoons all-purpose flour
5 tablespoons balsamic vinegar
2 cups brown ale

1 fresh bouquet garni (1 sprig of fresh thyme, 1 fresh bay
    leaf, and 2 to 3 parsley stalks, tied with kitchen twine)
Sea salt and freshly ground black pepper

FOR THE CROUTONS
2 tablespoons (¼ stick) softened butter
2 tablespoons Dijon mustard
1 tablespoon fresh thyme leaves
1 (10½-ounce) ciabatta loaf, cut into 8 to 10 slices

1 Remove any unwanted sinew or large bits of fat from the meat, but don't be too perfect about this—you want some fat remaining to enhance the flavor of the stew. Blot the meat on paper towels; this will help prevent it sticking to the bottom of the saucepan.

2 Preheat the oven to 350°F. In a large casserole dish, heat a good splash of oil. Add the meat in batches and seal the edges over high heat. Don't rush this step; it will make the stew taste all the richer. As each piece is done, remove, and set aside, adding a little more oil to the pot if needed.

3 Add more oil and sauté the onions and garlic until they are tinged with gold and have softened, 3 to 4 minutes. Return the beef shank to the pan. Sprinkle over the flour

and stir until it's disappeared. Pour in the balsamic vinegar followed by the ale. Top up with water so the liquid is just covering the meat and add the bouquet garni. Season. Cover with a tight-fitting lid and pop into the oven for 2½ to 3 hours. Check the dish every hour or so to make sure it isn't drying out—top up with a little water if necessary.

4 Meanwhile, make the croutons. Combine the softened butter with the mustard and thyme and generously slather over the slices of bread. When the shank has done its time, remove the lid and pop the mustard croutons on the surface, butter-side up. Return to the oven, covered, for another 20 minutes. Serve and enjoy.

SLOW-COOKED VEAL
& RED WINE STEW

When winter sets in and cold air covers the country like a carpet, I crave warming stews. Here, slabs of veal shank are cooked by a similar method to the well-known one-pot, osso bucco. Literally translated, "osso bucco" means "bone with a hole," which refers to the piece of bone encasing an ample amount of rich marrow in its center. During the lengthy cooking, the marrow melts into the sauce, leaving an open hole—thus the name (and an exceptionally tasty sauce). It is possible to source humanely reared veal, so you can indulge in this stew with a clear conscience. Enjoy piled on a mound of buttery mashed potatoes.

PREP TIME 40 MINUTES   SERVES 4   COOK TIME 2 HOURS

3 tablespoons extra virgin olive oil

4 (7- to 10½-ounce) veal shanks, bone in

3 medium onions, each cut into 8 wedges

8 garlic cloves, peeled and thickly sliced

1½ teaspoons ground cinnamon

2 tablespoons all-purpose flour

2 tablespoons tomato paste

1¼ cups medium-bodied red wine

¾ cup beef stock

14 ounces tomatoes, chopped

3 sprigs of rosemary

1 (15-ounce) can kidney beans, drained and rinsed

Sea salt and freshly ground black pepper

Fresh flat-leaf parsley, to garnish

Mashed potatoes, to serve

1 In a large, heavy-bottom pot, heat 2 tablespoons of the oil over medium heat. Cook each of the veal shanks until they start to caramelize, about 4 minutes each side. Remove them from the pot and set aside.

2 Add the remaining oil to the pot and sauté the onions over gentle heat until soft. Be careful not to let them catch—the burned taste will come through in the final dish. Add the garlic and cinnamon to the pot and cook, over lower heat, for another minute.

3 Return the veal to the pot and sprinkle over the flour. Stir through the tomato paste and combine until the flour

has all but disappeared. Pour over the wine, turn up the heat, and let the wine to bubble so the alcohol disappears.

4 Return the heat to low and add the beef stock, chopped tomatoes, and rosemary. Season vigorously before covering and cooking until the veal is perfectly tender and the marrow has melted into the sauce, about 2 hours.

5 Stir in the kidney beans and warm through for a few minutes before serving dressed with fresh parsley, atop a heap of creamy mashed potatoes.

BONED LAMB SHOULDER
WITH WALNUT & MINT PESTO

As a child I disliked pesto, but as an adult I put away my childish ways. Pesto is now an absolute staple in my kitchen. A riot of flavors, it can be used to spice up any dressing, sandwich, or, in this case, a heavenly hunk of lamb. If you are skilled with a butcher's knife, you can bone your own shoulder, but a quicker choice might be to ask the butcher kindly and watch in admiration as he delicately dances around the lamb, leaving you with not a bone in sight.

PREP TIME 20 MINUTES   SERVES 6   COOK TIME APPROX. 1 HOUR 40 MINUTES

1¾-pound boned shoulder of lamb (weight of meat without shoulder bone)
1 small red onion, thinly sliced
2 tablespoons olive oil
1½ pounds carrots, scrubbed and cut into 1¼-inch slices
1½ pounds potatoes, scrubbed and large ones cut in half
Sea salt and freshly ground black pepper

FOR THE PESTO
A (approx. 1 ounce) bunch of mint
½ bunch (approx. ¼ ounce) of flat-leaf parsley
3 garlic cloves, peeled
⅔ cup walnut halves
4 tablespoons extra virgin olive oil
½ teaspoon sea salt flakes

1 First, make the pesto. This is easy. Simply blend everything in a food processor, drizzling the oil in as you blitz. You want the pesto to be quite stiff, so refrain from adding any extra oil.

2 Preheat the oven to 425°F. Spread the lamb wide open on a board, then slather it with the pesto and sprinkle over the red onion. Season well.

3 Using a long piece of kitchen twine (I've used cotton in the absence of twine before), tie the shoulder up into a watermelon shape. Season the outside and drizzle with olive oil—don't go overboard, as the lamb will leech oil as it roasts. Calculate the cooking time at 20 minutes per pound plus 20 minutes.

4 Roast in the oven for 20 minutes before dropping the temperature down to 375°F for the remainder of the cooking time.

5 Forty minutes before the end of the cooking time, nestle the carrots and potatoes into the pan. Coat in any oil that has escaped from the lamb.

6 When the lamb's ready, remove the twine and place the meat on a warmed serving dish. Let rest for 15 minutes before serving.

LAMB SHANKS
WITH ANCHOVY & FETA

The lamb shank is a cut that appeals for many reasons: first, each bone supports a hunk of flavorful meat, plenty to satisfy any appetite; second, enough fat is hidden among the tendons to produce a gloriously rich sauce; third, it doesn't cost a fortune; and lastly, even the most nervous of cooks couldn't muddle this up—your dinner will taste delicious.

PREP TIME 30 MINUTES | SERVES 4 TO 6 | COOK TIME 3½ HOURS

2 tablespoons olive oil

4 (approx. 14-ounce) lamb shanks

2 onions, coarsely chopped

1 tablespoon tomato paste

2 teaspoons ground sumac

1½ ounces canned anchovies, drained and coarsely chopped

1 whole head of garlic, outer papery leaves removed and the bulb cut in half horizontally

1¾ pounds potatoes, scrubbed clean and cut into 1½-inch chunks

1¾ ounces fresh oregano, tied into a bundle with kitchen twine, plus extra to serve

2 cups hot lamb stock

1 cup red wine

Freshly ground black pepper

⅓ cup crumbled feta cheese, to serve

1 Preheat the oven to 325°F.

2 In a 6⅓-quart casserole dish, heat the olive oil and brown two shanks at a time, turning each shank regularly until the meat is evenly golden brown. Spend a good 10 minutes doing this; it is a good investment in your dish. Remove the shanks and set aside.

3 Add the onions to the pan and sauté until lightly golden, 3 to 4 minutes. Stir through the tomato paste and sumac and heat through for a minute.

4 Add the chopped anchovies and head of garlic, and heat through for a minute or so before adding the potatoes and

oregano bundle. Return the lamb shanks to the pot and pour over the lamb stock and red wine. Season with pepper only—there will be enough salt from the anchovies.

5 Cover with a lid and cook in the oven, undisturbed, until the lamb is trying to escape from the bone and the liquid has reduced, 2½ to 3 hours. Remove the lid for the final 30 minutes of cooking if you think the sauce could be a little thicker.

6 Remove from the oven and let cool slightly before sprinkling over the feta and fresh oregano. Serve with tzatziki, if you like—homemade is best!

FOUR-HOUR
LAMB SHOULDER

Tender lamb falling apart with a gentle nudge from the back of a spoon must be any carnivore's fantasy (certainly mine). Serve with something fresh to lighten the plate—crème fraîche and some well-seasoned greens for example. Just a thought… you can also run a marathon in four hours. Both activities might require an afternoon nap and a glass of red wine afterward!

PREP TIME 20 MINUTES   SERVES 6   COOK TIME 4 HOURS

1 shoulder of lamb (approx. 4½ pounds), bone in, trimmed of excess fat

3 or 4 rosemary sprigs

2 heads of garlic, cloves peeled and papery skin removed

2 red onions, each cut into 6 crescents

2 large carrots, peeled and sliced into 1-inch rounds

2 turnips, peeled and cut into chunks

2 (14½-ounce) cans diced tomatoes

2 fresh bay leaves

2 cups red wine

Sea salt and freshly ground black pepper

1 Preheat the oven to 325°F.

2 Prepare your lamb by making 10 to 15 incisions all over the top of the meat. Poke peeled garlic cloves and sprigs of rosemary into the holes, then season well all over.

3 Place the onions, carrots, and turnips in the bottom of the roasting pan and nestle the lamb on top. Add the chopped tomatoes, bay leaves, and red wine to the pan. Season again.

4 Cover with a sheet of parchment paper and then foil, and place in the oven. Cook for 2 hours.

5 Reduce the heat to 300°F. Remove the foil and paper from the lamb, baste the meat, and return to the oven to cook for another 2 hours (check after 1½ hours in case you have a ferocious oven). The lamb will be ready when the meat is falling away from the bone. Skim off the fat and serve directly from the roasting pan.

LAMB STEW
WITH ARTICHOKES & SQUASHED TOMATOES

Slow cooking often takes me by surprise. After a few hours of close confinement, seemingly individual ingredients grow fond of one another and unite in a flavor that exceeds expectations. Here the lamb is steeped with lemon and artichokes, a traditionally Greek combination that I love. Mint and parsley chopped on top give a perfectly fresh finish, and my vote would be for a spoonful of polenta, too.

PREP TIME 25 MINUTES   SERVES 4   COOK TIME 2½ HOURS

3 tablespoons olive oil

2¼ pounds lean shoulder of lamb, cut into 1¼-inch cubes

1 large onion, coarsely chopped

4 garlic cloves, peeled and thinly sliced

2 tablespoons red wine vinegar

1¼ cups red wine

1 tablespoon tomato paste

1 (14½-ounce) can diced tomatoes

1 (14-ounce) can or jar marinated artichoke hearts

Grated zest of 1 lemon and 2 tablespoons lemon juice

1 (15-ounce) can cannellini beans, drained and rinsed

Sea salt and freshly ground black pepper

Fresh mint and flat-leaf parsley, to garnish

1 Preheat the oven to 325°F. In a deep casserole dish, heat 2 tablespoons of the olive oil over high heat and brown the lamb pieces in batches until each is well colored. Transfer to a bowl and set aside.

2 Reduce the heat to medium and add the remaining olive oil. Add the onion to the pot and sauté until it is tender and soft, 3 to 4 minutes. Add the garlic for the last couple of minutes. Return the lamb to the pot.

3 Turn the heat up and pour over the vinegar. Cook until it has almost evaporated, then add ⅓ cup of the wine, the tomato paste, and diced tomatoes. Season with pinches of salt and plenty of grinds of black pepper. Cover with a lid and pop in the oven for 1¾ hours.

4 Remove from the oven and stir in the artichokes, lemon zest and juice, cannellini beans, and remaining wine (if you think a little more liquid is needed). Return to the oven and cook for another 30 minutes with no lid.

5 Serve sprinkled liberally with the fresh parsley and mint.

 TIP—TO MAKE POLENTA: BRING 3⅓ TO 4 CUPS DELICIOUS CHICKEN STOCK TO A BOIL IN A MEDIUM-SIZE POT. SLOWLY POUR IN 1¼ CUPS INSTANT POLENTA AND STIR AS QUICKLY AS YOUR WRISTS ALLOW TO BEAT OUT THE LUMPS. BUBBLE THE POLENTA FOR A FEW MINUTES, STIRRING, UNTIL THICKENED. REMOVE FROM THE HEAT, STIR IN 3 TABLESPOONS BUTTER AND ½ CUP FINELY GRATED PARMESAN CHEESE. SEASON, SEASON, SEASON, AND SERVE. DELICIOUS.

TENDER LAMB MEATBALLS
WITH CORN & BALSAMIC

In my opinion, meatballs have suffered from school-dinner syndrome and, as a result, have an undeservedly poor reputation, but they can be sophisticated and punchy. Here, I've simply added cumin and fresh herbs to ground lamb and I think it's made all the difference… it's the small things. Serve with rice or chunks of bread.

PREP TIME 15 MINUTES   SERVES 4   COOK TIME 45 MINUTES

18 ounces ground lamb

2 tablespoons coarsely chopped flat-leaf parsley

1 teaspoon ground cumin

2 to 3 tablespoons vegetable oil

FOR THE SAUCE

1 large onion, coarsely chopped

3 garlic cloves, peeled and sliced

½ teaspoon cumin seed

2 (14½-ounce) cans diced tomatoes

2 tablespoons balsamic vinegar

1 tablespoon brown sugar

2 corn on the cob, 1 with the kernels stripped off and
    1 cut into 5 to 6 equal chunks

2 tablespoons coarsely chopped flat-leaf parsley

Sea salt and freshly ground black pepper

1 First off, make the meatballs. Put the lamb into a medium-size bowl with the ground cumin and parsley and use your hands to combine thoroughly. Season. Make 10 to 12 balls, each about the size of a golf ball.

2 In a flameproof casserole dish or deep-sided skillet, heat the vegetable oil and cook the meatballs on all sides, wiggling as you go to brown all over. You may have to do this in batches. When they are ready, remove them from the pan.

3 For the sauce, turn the heat down slightly, add a splash more oil, throw the onion and garlic into the pan, and cook until translucent, about 4 minutes. Add the cumin seed and cook for another couple of minutes.

4 Pour in the diced tomatoes and either chop up a bit more with a wooden spoon in the pan or just leave them as they are. Add the vinegar and sugar and bring to a simmer.

5 Lower the heat and return the meatballs to the pan. Cook, covered, on low heat for about 20 minutes. Add the corn chunks and kernels and simmer for a final 10 minutes without the lid on.

6 Just before serving, check the seasoning and freshen up with some chopped parsley.

MINT & RED CURRANT

LAMB WITH BEANS

We all have people who have been an inspiration to us and mine is Milla. She was the catalyst to my love of cooking, and together we can paw over cookbooks and discuss restaurants late into the night. It was during one such session in Norfolk, in the East of England, that we developed this recipe. The red currant jelly slowly melts while the fresh mint lightens the lamb. One note before you begin: it may seem like a lot of beans but, trust us, the quantities complement each other.

PREP TIME 20 MINUTES   SERVES 6   COOK TIME 2 HOURS

3¾- to 4½-pound leg of lamb

4 garlic cloves, peeled but kept whole

1 good sprig of rosemary

2 tablespoons olive oil

2 heaping tablespoons coarsely chopped mint

2 (14-ounce) cans flageolet beans, drained and rinsed

Heaping ⅓ cup red currant jelly, warmed

2⅔ cups cherry tomatoes

3 to 4 large zucchini, halved lengthwise and chopped into ½-inch crescents

⅓ cup vegetable stock

Sea salt and freshly ground black pepper

1 Preheat the oven to 400°F.

2 Make incisions all over your lamb by poking the tip of a knife through the skin. Rub the lamb all over with the garlic, then poke halved cloves and rosemary tufts into the incisions as though you're planting cuttings in the garden. Place in a deep roasting pan and drizzle over the olive oil.

3 Roast the lamb in the oven for 1 hour, until it's just starting to turn golden. Meanwhile, combine the chopped mint, flageolet beans, red currant jelly, cherry tomatoes, sliced zucchini, and stock. Season enthusiastically.

4 Remove the lamb from the oven briefly and spoon the bean mixture around the meat until it is surrounded by a sea of beans. Reduce the temperature to 350°F and return the meat to the oven for 1 hour, or until the lamb is cooked as you wish (a good test is that the meat has pulled away from the bone, leaving the top exposed).

5 Remove the lamb from the beans and let the meat rest for 10 minutes before carving. This is the moment when you can add a bit more stock to the beans if you think it's needed. Season and spoon onto hot plates with a good hunk of lamb.

 TIP—I LIKE A BIT MORE FRESH CHOPPED MINT STIRRED THROUGH THE BEANS JUST BEFORE SERVING.

LAMB TAGINE

Perhaps one of the most distinguished cooking vessels, the traditional African tagine towers majestically over other plain-looking pots. Yet the design is not simply beautiful; it serves a purpose and adds to the dish. You see, steam rises up inside the conical lid and recondenses before trickling back down the side of the pot and into the stew, keeping it moist and saucy. With water shortages rife in Africa, every little drop is conserved and appreciated. Of course, if you don't happen to have a tagine handy, a sturdy casserole dish does the job perfectly. Serve this lamb tagine with toasted couscous (see tip below) and a glass of fresh mint tea.

PREP TIME 20 MINUTES   SERVES 6   COOK TIME 2 HOURS

1 tablespoon olive oil

3-pound shoulder or leg of lamb, cut into 1-inch cubes

2 onions, coarsely chopped

1 large piece of fresh ginger, peeled and chopped

3 garlic cloves, peeled and each cut into 2

1 cinnamon stick

2 teaspoons ground coriander

1 teaspoon ground cumin

1 teaspoon ground allspice

5½ ounces Medjool dates, pitted and coarsely chopped if they are large ones

A trickle of honey

1 (14½-ounce) can diced tomatoes

Thinly pared zest of 1 lemon (use a vegetable peeler)

1¼ cups lamb stock

Sea salt and freshly ground black pepper

1 In a 4¼-quart, heavy-bottom pot, heat 1 tablespoon olive oil. Season the lamb and cook in batches, on high heat, until the pieces have begun to brown on all sides. Remove from the pan and set aside.

2 Reduce the heat to low and add a little more oil to the pan if needed. Gently sauté the onions, ginger, and garlic until softened, 5 to 10 minutes. Add the cinnamon stick, ground coriander, cumin, and allspice and combine well. Take a moment to breathe in the spell of the spices.

3 Return the browned lamb to the pot, then add the dates, honey, diced tomatoes, lemon zest, and lamb stock. Season and bring to a boil, cover with a lid, and cook on low heat for 1½ hours, by which time the lamb should be beautifully tender. Remove the lid and cook so the juice becomes syrupy, another 10 minutes.

TIP—TAGINES ARE DELICIOUS SERVED WITH COUSCOUS. TO MAKE YOUR COUSCOUS ALL THE MORE FLAVORSOME, DRY-TOAST IT FIRST—SIMPLY PUT A HEAVY-BOTTOMED SKILLET ON THE HEAT AND ADD THE GRANULES. KEEP TOSSING THEM AROUND THE PAN UNTIL THEY START TO TURN GOLDEN. ADD THE STOCK AND CARRY ON AS USUAL. THE COUSCOUS WILL HAVE DEVELOPED A DISTINCT NUTTY TASTE THAT GIVES A BIT MORE DEPTH.

PERFECT POTS *of* DESSERT

Some of us are just born with a sweet tooth, and some of us aren't. Sadly for my thighs, I fit snugly into the first category and as such need to punctuate every meal with a sweet exclamation mark.

It might also be that in my world desserts often mean an end-of-meal game. Here's one of my friend Sam's inventions: movie tennis, which should last as long as it takes to eat an ice cream sundae. Divide any diners into two teams and decide on a famous movie star. Next, and it is this simple, each team takes a turn in naming a movie in which this star has played a part. Keep batting the answers back and forth until one team triumphs with better movie knowledge!

Please also note that I've deviated with my one-pot desserts just a tiny bit. It seems a bit trickier to make desserts in one pot, but they are still simple as can be. And some of the recipes aren't served in one pot, but it's always nice to be given your own serving—it makes it very clear what is yours and there is no chance of anybody doing any stealing.

PEACH, MINT
& BRIOCHE TRIFLE

Trifle strikes me as a festive dessert, a frivolous combination of all things naughty that sits overnight, bonding next to the mince pies and thawing turkey. But here we have a recipe for summer trifle that rivals its Christmas counterpart with fresh ingredients—a hint of sweet and the obligatory dusting of alcohol. Serve with ice-cold Pimm's, a rum punch, or even a glass of chilled wine.

PREP TIME 15 MINUTES   SERVES 10   CHILL TIME 3 HOURS

6 finger brioche rolls (or 6 slices from a brioche loaf)

Scant ⅓ cup raspberry jam

⅓ cup sweet wine

2 cups ready-made vanilla custard or custard dessert

1 cup extra-thick heavy cream (or heavy cream whipped to stiff peaks)

2 tablespoons confectioners' sugar, sifted, plus extra for dusting

2 small ripe peaches, pitted and cut into slices

1⅔ cups beautiful fresh raspberries

2 tablespoons finely chopped mint, plus extra leaves to decorate

¼ cup coarsely chopped pistachios

1 Slice the brioche rolls through the center horizontally and spread half of them with raspberry jam. Sandwich together with their other halves and then cut each mini loaf into lots of ½-inch slices. Arrange half of the slices attractively in the base of 10 wine glasses or a 2-quart glass serving dish. Sprinkle the sweet wine over the brioche.

2 In a small bowl, combine the custard and cream and sweeten with the confectioners' sugar. Drop half of the mixture in spoonfuls over the brioche. Arrange nearly all of the peach slices and half of the raspberries over the custard mixture, then dust with a little finely chopped mint.

3 Now you do it all again in a second layer. Start with the brioche slices, then custard mixture, and finally the remaining raspberries, peach slices, and mint. Finish off with the chopped pistachios.

4 Chill for at least 3 hours and then serve triumphantly dusted with confectioners' sugar and decorated with extra mint leaves.

PLUM TARTE TATIN

The French have a knack for creating tarts that set the benchmark for desserts, and the classic tarte tatin is no exception. Buying ready-made puff pastry is the cook's bonus—you don't have to be a pastry chef to make this one turn out perfectly.

PREP TIME 25 MINUTES   **SERVES 6**   COOK TIME 30 MINUTES

18 ounces puff pastry dough

All-purpose flour, for dusting

3 tablespoons unsalted butter

½ cup light brown sugar

1 vanilla bean, seeds removed (optional)

2 tablespoons amaretto (optional)

14 ounces firm red plums (enough to cover the base of the pan), cut into halves and pitted

1 Preheat the oven to 425°F.

2 Roll out the puff pastry on a lightly floured surface and cut out a 10½-inch circle. Place in the fridge and chill while you make the rest of the tart.

3 Melt the butter in a 9½-inch ovenproof skillet. Add the sugar, vanilla seeds, and amaretto (if using) and melt over medium/low heat. Shake the pan gently but do not stir, and let bubble for a minute.

4 Arrange the plums, cut-side down, on top of the caramel in a spiral pattern. Cover with the prepared pastry circle and tuck the edges inside the pan around the plums.

5 Place in the oven and bake for 30 minutes, or until the pastry is golden brown and puffed up. Remove from the oven and let cool for 10 minutes before inverting a serving plate over the pan and flipping over as fast as your arms allow. Serve warm with cream.

 TIP—THIS IS A GREAT DESSERT FOR PREPARING IN ADVANCE. MAKE THE WHOLE LOT—I.E. THE CARAMEL WITH PLUMS PATIENTLY SITTING AND THE PUFF PASTRY CIRCLE TUCKED ON TOP—AND LEAVE ASIDE. JUST POP IN THE OVEN 40 MINUTES BEFORE YOU WANT TO SERVE.

MOMMA'S BLUEBERRY

& VANILLA STEAMED SPONGE

Something wonderful happens when a cake batter is cooked with steam whereby the texture is transformed to a moist honeycomb. I have to hand over the credit for this recipe to my mother who puffs, proud as a peacock, every time this dessert hits the table.

PREP TIME 20 MINUTES · SERVES 6 TO 8 · COOK TIME 2 HOURS

¾ cup softened butter, plus a little extra for greasing

¾ cup plus 1 heaping tablespoon superfine sugar

Grated zest of 1 lemon

1 teaspoon vanilla extract

3 medium free-range eggs, lightly beaten

⅔ cup blueberries

1 tablespoon all-purpose flour

1⅓ cups self-rising flour

½ teaspoon baking powder

Golden syrup or dark corn syrup, to serve

1 Grease a 5-cup bundt pan liberally with butter.

2 In a medium-size bowl, cream together the butter and sugar until pale and light. Stir in the lemon zest and vanilla extract, then slowly add the beaten eggs.

3 Lightly wash the blueberries in water, drain off any excess water, then sprinkle the all-purpose flour over the fruit.

4 Fold the self-rising flour and baking powder through the creamed mixture and finally fold through the floury blueberries (the flour on the outside will help them cling to the batter and not all sink to the bottom).

5 Spoon the mixture into the bundt pan and cover with greased foil, making a pleat in the foil across the top of the bowl. Tie firmly with kitchen twine.

6 Steam for 2 hours, until risen. If you don't own a steamer, put an upturned saucer in a deep pan (this will act as a trivet) and rest your bundt pan on the top. Add cold water until it's about a quarter of the way up the bowl. Put the pan on the heat and bring to a boil. Lower the temperature and keep topping up with water, more often than you think, every 20 to 25 minutes, to make sure there is constant steam.

7 To serve, run a knife round the sides of the pan, turn out, and lavishly smother syrup on the top.

 TIP—IF YOU UNVEIL YOUR SPONGE AND FEAR THAT IT MAY NOT BE COOKED THROUGH IN THE CENTER (PERHAPS A LITTLE WATER HAS TUNNELED ITS WAY INSIDE), GIVE IT 30 SECONDS ON HIGH IN THE MICROWAVE. NOT THE BEST, I KNOW, BUT WHEN THERE ARE SIX HUNGRY PEOPLE WAITING FOR THEIR DESSERT...

BANANA BREAD
& BUTTER PUDDDING

Some desserts are a throwback to school days and this is certainly one. More often than not the memories of bread and butter pudding need to be banished and erased… and then reinvented. This recipe is a super-speedy version that doesn't require a premade custard; it is, as you'd expect, a one-pot version. A rustic crust hides wobbly custard, while flecks of fruit offer familiar comfort; all that's needed is a blob of ice cream gently melting by its side.

PREP TIME 15 MINUTES
(PLUS 30 MINUTES SOAKING)

SERVES 6

COOK TIME 40 MINUTES

2 tablespoons (¼ stick) softened unsalted butter,
  plus extra for greasing
6 slices of crusty white bread
2 medium free-range eggs
1¾ cups plus 2 tablespoons whole milk
2 tablespoons light brown sugar, plus 2 tablespoons
  extra for the crunchy top

1 teaspoon vanilla extract
Grated zest of 1 lemon
2 to 3 very ripe bananas (nearly brown is just fine),
  cut lengthwise into ¼-inch strips
¼ cup juicy raisins (optional)
Ice cream, to serve

1 Lightly grease a 1-quart ovenproof dish.

2 Spread the bread lightly with butter and cut diagonally in half to form triangles.

3 Crack the eggs into a medium bowl and beat lightly for a minute or so using a hand mixer. Pour over the milk and continue to beat for another minute. Stir through the sugar, vanilla, and lemon zest and beat to combine.

4 Now there's the arranging. Place the buttered triangles into the dish with the longest side touching the bottom so they look like mountains. Arrange a triangle of bread at one end, then a banana slither, then bread, and so on until you see a mountain range forming. It's easiest to fill both

ends of the dish and where both ends meet in the center, curl the bread and banana to fit the space.

5 Gently pour over the milk mixture, taking care to cover each piece of bread, and let sit for 30 minutes. Preheat the oven to 350°F.

6 Scatter the pudding with raisins (if using) and the extra 2 tablespoons brown sugar. Fill a roasting pan halfway up with water to make a bain-marie and place the pudding in the center. Bake in the oven for 35 to 40 minutes. Remove from the oven and let stand for a few minutes before serving with ice-cold ice cream.

RASPBERRY, ALMOND
& APPLE JUMBLE

Possibly my new favorite. Tart fruit, dense custard, and pastry married in their own little pastry pot. Ticks the dessert box very prettily, very prettily indeed.

PREP TIME 15 MINUTES   SERVES 6   COOK TIME 30 MINUTES

All-purpose flour, for dusting

18 ounces puff pastry dough

2 tablespoons custard powder

½ cup superfine sugar

1 cup ground almonds

1 medium free-range egg

14 ounces baking apples (approx. 2), peeled, cored, and thinly sliced

Scant 1 cup fresh raspberries

1 tablespoon whole milk, for brushing

1 tablespoon dark brown sugar

1 tablespoon flaked almonds

Heavy cream, to serve

1 Preheat the oven to 375°F.

2 Dust the work surface lightly with flour and roll out the puff pastry until it's approximately ¼ inch thick. Cut out a 12-inch circle (I'd find a large plate or pan lid to trace around with a knife) and slide this onto a cookie sheet.

3 In a small bowl, mix your custard powder, ¼ cup of the superfine sugar, the ground almonds, and egg. Stir until you have a thick paste.

4 Spread the almond paste in the center of your circle of pastry, leaving a good 2½ inches around the edge. Pile the apple slices and raspberries on top of the paste.

5 Now comes the moment where you create your own pastry pot! Brush the 2½-inch border with milk and gather the dough edge around your fruit pile so you can still see lots of fruit in the center. Brush the outside of the pastry with a little more milk and pop into the oven.

6 Bake your pie for 20 minutes. Remove from the oven and sprinkle over the brown sugar and flaked almonds. Return to the oven for another 10 minutes. Serve in slices with a good splash of cold, fresh heavy cream swimming on the side.

PASSION FRUIT
& LEMON CURD POTS

Such a deliciously simple dessert to put together and a good one for those messy chefs who like flinging ingredients into a bowl. I've used passion fruit, but you can try any fruit that is in season—such as raspberries, strawberries, poached rhubarb, or stewed apple and cinnamon—for an equally successful dish.

PREP TIME 15 MINUTES · SERVES 6 · FREEZING TIME 1 HOUR

Heaping ¾ cup good-quality lemon curd

Thinly pared zest and juice of 1 large lemon

2 cups thickly set Greek yogurt

3½ ounces gingersnaps or shortbread, lightly crumbled into ½-inch pieces

3 passion fruits

¼ cup coarsely chopped pistachios

You will also need 6 (5-ounce) glass dishes

1 In a small bowl, mix the lemon curd with a little lemon juice so the consistency becomes that of thick molasses. Stir a little water or milk into the yogurt if it's too thick—the consistency should be the same as the lemon mixture.

2 Drop alternate spoonfuls of lemon mixture, yogurt (reserving a little for the top), crushed cookies, and passion fruit pulp into each of the 6 glass dishes.

Don't worry about being too neat; this is a jumbled dessert, which improves if it's a bit messy.

3 Top with a blob of the reserved yogurt, chopped pistachios, and a swirl of lemon zest, then freeze for just 1 hour: don't let the yogurt become too solid. Serve with a silver teaspoon.

 TIP—IF YOU HAVE MADE THESE IN ADVANCE, LET THE DESSERTS "COME TO" IN A COOL AREA (NO NEED TO REFRIGERATE) FOR 2 HOURS OR SO BEFORE SERVING. IT WILL MAKE THEM EASIER TO ATTACK.

MUSCAT, CHERRY
& APPLE JELLY

A most delicate and pretty dessert that captures fruit in crystal-clear suspension and suggests cooking prowess by any host who is able to deliver. One word of warning: many cooks get nervous at the gelatin moment, tossing up whether to add more than the instructions suggest, "just to be safe." My advice? Don't do it; a soft-set jelly trumps any bouncy-ball equivalent and the package directions are generally right.

PREP TIME 20 MINUTES — SERVES 4 — SETTING TIME 4 TO 5 HOURS

4 sheets of leaf gelatin (enough to set approx. 2¼ cups)
12½ fl oz-bottle of Muscat (or any other sweet wine)
1 tablespoon superfine sugar
⅔ cup sparkling mineral water

1¼ cups cherries, pitted, plus 4 extra to decorate
½ small green apple, cored and thinly sliced

You will also need 4 (9-ounce) stemmed glasses

1 Soak the gelatin in cold water for 5 minutes or so. The texture of the sheets will change from that of solid glass window panes to pliable, see-through jelly. Remove from the liquid and squeeze with your hands to remove as much liquid as possible.

2 Pour the Muscat into a pan and heat gently, but do not let simmer. Remove from the heat and add the sugar. Stir until it has dissolved and add the softened gelatin sheets until they have all but disappeared. Stir through the sparkling water.

3 Let the mixture cool slightly, about 10 minutes—this will help the fruit to be suspended in your glasses rather than just float to the top.

4 Place a dense cluster of cherries and apple at the bottom of each of your glasses and gently pour over a bit of the liquid. As the fruit begins to float, stop and place the glasses in the fridge.

5 After about 1 hour, when the fruits no longer bob to the surface, pour the remaining jelly over the fruit. Let set for 3 to 4 hours. Decorate with the reserved whole cherries before serving.

POMEGRANATE

& PISTACHIO RICE PUDDING

It always surprises me that tiny grains of pudding rice drink far more than their body weight in creamy milk. The quantities seem unlikely when you first put them in the pan, but with love and persistence all that liquid is soaked up. You're left with the most beautiful of puddings—a snowy-white mountain, kissed with molasses and the greens and reds of pistachios and pomegranates.

PREP TIME 10 MINUTES   SERVES 4   COOK TIME 45 MINUTES

½ cup dry short-grain white rice, rinsed under cold running water

Heaping ⅓ cup superfine sugar

Grated zest of 2 lemons

3⅓ to 4 cups whole milk

2 tablespoons pomegranate molasses

2 tablespoons fresh pomegranate seeds

¼ cup coarsely chopped pistachios

1 Place the rice, sugar, lemon zest, and milk in a saucepan. Bring to a boil over medium heat, stirring occasionally. Reduce the heat and simmer, stirring frequently, until the rice is soft and swollen and the milk is absorbed, about 35 minutes. Add a little more milk if you think it's needed, as everyone's pudding will boil at a slightly different pace.

2 Serve immediately, drizzled with tart pomegranate molasses, the pomegranate seeds, and green pistachios.

MAPLE-BAKED OATS
WITH FIGS

Ideally, brunch suggests lazy mornings spent lazing in pajamas with lazy food that doesn't require too much tending. Here, you'll find a cross between a warming oatmeal and an English flapjack, with beautiful figs and delicate tart apple running through the oats. Common to most brunches, syrup is an absolute must! A brunch without maple is like a Mountie without his hat.

PREP TIME 10 MINUTES   SERVES 6   COOK TIME 35 TO 40 MINUTES

2 cups lowfat milk

2 medium free-range eggs

2 tablespoons (¼ stick) unsalted butter, melted

5 tablespoons maple syrup

4 tablespoons dark brown sugar

1 large baking apple, peeled, cored, and cut into
   ½-inch cubes

4 to 5 ripe figs, each cut into 8

2¼ cups rolled oats

1 heaping teaspoon baking powder

1 teaspoon ground allspice

A pinch of salt

½ cup slivered almonds

Yogurt, to serve

1 Preheat the oven to 350°F. Grease the bottom of a 1-quart ovenproof dish.

2 In a small bowl or pitcher, gently beat the milk, eggs, melted butter, maple syrup, and half of the sugar.

3 Tumble the chunks of apple and half of the figs into your dish with the oats, baking powder, allspice, and salt. Give everything a good jumble around using your hands or a large spoon. Gently pour over the milk mixture and let soak in for a few minutes.

4 Sprinkle the remaining figs, the slivered almonds, and the remaining sugar onto the mixture, then bake in the oven for 35 to 40 minutes, until the milk has become fully absorbed. Serve while still warm with yogurt for a delicious brunch dish.

3-MINUTE CHOCOLATE
MUG CAKE

Imagine the things you could do in three minutes: make a cup of tea, brush your teeth, listen to a Beatles song, make the bed, do a Sudoku, write a (probably not very good) haiku... And make a cake! Welcome to the world of microwave chocolate mug cake. I take no responsibility for the recipe, nor can I say that the result is the most complex, interesting cake; but nonetheless it definitely fills a hole.

PREP TIME 2 MINUTES   SERVES 2   COOK TIME 3 MINUTES

4 tablespoons all-purpose flour

4 tablespoons superfine sugar

2 tablespoons unsweetened cocoa

1 medium free-range egg

3 tablespoons lowfat milk

3 tablespoons vegetable oil

A small splash of vanilla or orange extract

Grated zest of 1 large orange

1 Place the dry ingredients in a bowl and mix well. Add the egg, stir, then pour in the milk and oil. Mix well again.

2 Add the vanilla/orange extract and orange zest and mix. Pour into two large mugs and cook in the microwave for 3 minutes at 1000 watts.

3 The cake might rise over the top of the mugs, but don't be afraid—the mixture will set. Let cool a little, then tip out onto plates and serve each cake with a good spoonful of good-quality ice cream.

SEXY COFFEE
& HAZELNUT POTS

There is a reason why these tiny pots are but two or three mouthfuls—you couldn't, or at least shouldn't, eat too much more. Your thighs wouldn't thank you.

PREP TIME 10 MINUTES   **SERVES 8**   COOK TIME 15 MINUTES

¾ cup plus 1 heaping tablespoon superfine sugar

¾ cup unsweetened powder

⅓ cup plus 1 tablespoon all-purpose flour

2 medium free-range eggs

2 cups lowfat milk

1 teaspoon instant coffee granules

A handful of hazelnuts, skin on

You will need 8 (3½-ounce) pots

1 Put the sugar, cocoa, and all-purpose flour into a large saucepan and make a well in the center.

2 Crack your eggs into the well and stir, gradually incorporating the dry ingredients to form a chocolaty paste. Slowly add the milk and beat with a wooden spoon until all is added. Stir though the coffee.

3 Place the saucepan on low heat (don't be tempted to increase the heat or the eggs will cook too quickly and you will be left with scrambled eggs) and continue to stir until the mixture has thickened and is beginning to form small lumps on the spoon, about 15 minutes. The consistency should be that of extra-thick heavy cream.

4 Remove from the heat and, using a wire whip, beat out the lumps with enthusiastic vigor; they will disappear.

5 Divide the mixture among eight mugs, cups, or pots and scatter over the hazelnuts. Let set for a couple of hours before serving.

INDEX